gods of men:
End Time Awakening

OLADIPUPO JUDE MESOLE

gods of men: End Time Awakening

Copyright © 2022 by Oladipupo Jude Mesole

All rights reserved. No part of this book may be reproduced or transmitted in any form or by any means without the written permission of the author.

Scriptures marked KJV are taken from the KING JAMES VERSION (KJV): KING JAMES VERSION, public domain.

Scripture taken from the New King James Version®. Copyright © 1982 by Thomas Nelson. Used by permission. All rights reserved.

Scripture quotations marked (NIV) are taken from the Holy Bible, New International Version®, NIV®. Copyright © 1973, 1978, 1984, 2011 by Biblica, Inc.™ Used by permission of Zondervan. All rights reserved worldwide. www.zondervan.com. The "NIV" and "New International Version" are trademarks registered in the United States Patent and Trademark Office by Biblica, Inc.™.

Scriptures marked AMP are taken from the AMPLIFIED BIBLE (AMP): Scripture taken from the AMPLIFIED® BIBLE, Copyright © 1954, 1958, 1962, 1964, 1965, 1987 by the Lockman Foundation Used by Permission. (www.Lockman.org)

Published by:
Eleviv Publishing Group
Centerville, OH 45458
info@elevivpublishing.com
www.elevivpublishing.com

ISBN:
978-1-952744-58-7 (PB)
978-1-952744-48-8 (Ebook)

Printed in the United States of America

Dedication

I dedicate this book to God Almighty.

And to the memory of my late sister, Bolanle Mesole, who I was with on her last day on earth. She was knocked down in my presence by a speeding vehicle on the walkway of our estate in Ilorin, Kwara State, Nigeria, on May 11th, 1991.

To every sincere clergyperson who serves and still serves God in truth without exploitation.

To my wife and children and their future.

Acknowledgment

I acknowledge everyone bringing people's attention to the activities of false preachers all over the globe; their excellent job is well recognized and has been a motivation; despite their suppression, they remain resolute and trust in God.

I appreciate my parents, Chief James Otitoju & Elizabeth Remilekun Mesole, for the values they taught my siblings and me. Also, for being an example of good value and their unquantifiable investment in me through moral values, Christian doctrines, and financial investment in quality education.

I acknowledge my wife, her parents Mr.& Mrs. Gabriel, and my siblings for their encouragement and consistent show of love.

Introduction

I am so pained by how many Christians invest their time, energy, and resources in commitment to serving under a pastor who isn't on the right path with God. Some people are so lost in their minds that they cover up for them, such as lying-in defense and conspiring to deceive people through false testimonies and arranged miracles.

Some People will passionately invest time to service, turning blind eyes to all the things happening there, and some are unaware of those dubious activities. God is not in such a place where such happens, Ezekiel 13:1-4,

Then the word of the LORD came to me. He said, 2 "Son of man, [a] you must speak to the prophets of Israel for me. They are only saying what they want to say. You must speak to them. Tell them this: 'Listen to this message from the LORD! 3 This is what the Lord GOD says. Bad things will happen to you foolish prophets. You are following your own spirits. You are not telling people what you really see in visions.

4 "'Israel, your prophets are false prophets. They are like jackals hunting for food among the ruins of a city.

If the Bible declares that bad things will happen to them, their enablers will not escape.

I take joy in seeing Christians across the globe realize there is a need to build an intimate relationship with God and not depend on any man to mediate between God and them.

This book explains and reveals the devices of false prophets and how to identify them by their activities using biblical references concerning present-day life occurrences. The book will also discuss the influence of occultism on the Church, such as how False prophets acquire powers to deceive people to get fame and attract more gullible members.

Every Christian must know that we are responsible for our decisions and actions. Serving under a false prophet is the fault of anyone who finds themselves in that situation; this is because the Bible has warned us in many ways, even saying, *"By their fruits, you shall know them."* For you to know them by their fruits, you must have studied God's word and have a personal relationship with God. Your inability to do that as a person will be your fault; therefore, it is essential to be vigilant and watch against men busy building their business empires and claiming they are building for God.

Why the interest in creating an end-time awakening about the activities of the false prophets? There is a burden for the truth to be told about the happenings in the Church. Many souls have been kept in bondage and psychologically destabilized; these gods of men have driven many people into depression through their style of taking people's intellectual, financial, and time value. This book will equip readers with the tools to break free from the bondage of these monsters decorated as Men of God. God has given us His word to live by and learn from; our focus must be on seeking His face, not a mere man's face. We are called to love God and serve Him and not to waste our years running after shadows dished out by so-called prophets. I employ you to find God for yourself and let Him be your guide. As you read this book, I pray that your spiritual eyes be open, and may you have wisdom in your pursuit of God and your Christian walk.

Shalom

Table of Content

Dedication

Acknowledgment

Introduction

01. Broken Cisterns in the House of God.... *9*
02. Bearers of the Fruits of Deceits.... *23*
03. Occultic influence in the church.... *37*
04. An Exposition of Matthew Chapter Five.... *50*
05. An Exposition on Galatian Chapter Six.... *66*
06. The Holy Spirit.... *78*
07. Religious Malpractice and National Development: Nigeria as a case study. How Religious Malpractice Has Affected the Peace of Nigeria.... *93*
08. Alliance Between the False Prophets and Authorities in Power.... *105*
09. Has God Really Spoken?.... *117*
10. Morals Should Count for Something.... *135*
11. Turn Your Eyes Upon Jesus.... *152*
12. The simplicity of the Gospel of Christ.... *168*
13. Laziness Knows Them by Name.... *180*

Conclusion

About the author

Chapter One

Broken Cisterns in the House of God.

This know also, that in the last days perilous times shall come. For men shall be lovers of their own selves, covetous, boasters, proud, blasphemers, disobedient to parents, unthankful, unholy, Having a form of godliness, but denying the power thereof: from such turn away. 2 Timothy 3:1-2, 5 (KJV).

The existence of false prophets in Christianity today cannot be denied. Many preachers in Christian churches today preach the word of God but with a selfish motive rather than what God expects of his representatives among His children.

Many of these false prophets or preachers exhibit their falsehood in several forms, highlighting their dubious nature to those spiritually sensitive. Unfortunately, several ignorant Christians unknowingly fall headlong into the traps of these dry wells with no water.

The scripture prepares our minds for what to expect from such false preachers. 2 Timothy 3:1-2 tells us what men would be like in the last days. The description above does not exempt the so-called men of God. The spirit of selfishness and covetousness will consume many, including some men of God who might have started their walk with God with good intentions. The result is that they end badly.

2 Timothy 3:5 describes certain people of the last days as having a form of godliness but denying the power thereof. Many of these false prophets are outwardly righteous-looking, spic and span. They are the ones who want to put on all-white apparel anytime they are in public, but outward appearance means little to God. Who we are on the inside is what God is interested in. *(But the LORD said unto Samuel, Look not on his countenance, or on the height of his stature; because I have refused him: for the LORD seeth not as man seeth; for man looketh on the outward appearance, but the LORD looketh on the heart. 1 Samuel 16:7).*

Also, many false prophets parade themselves as God's mouthpiece but cannot perform the miracles Christ said His followers would perform. They, therefore, deny the power in Christ by failing upcoming Christians with little faith who look unto them as the express image of God.

The instruction that ended *2 Timothy 3:5* cannot be misinterpreted or misquoted. The meaning is clear to any right-minded person. 'From such, turn away.' Christ expects us to turn away from such false representatives of God.

In *2 Corinthians 6:14 (KJV), the Bible says: Be ye not unequally yoked together with unbelievers: for what fellowship hath righteousness with unrighteousness? and what communion hath light with darkness?* It refers not only to those who blatantly oppose God but also false prophets, wolves in sheep's skin. It also expects us not to share in their burden or yoke. This verse hints that those who continue to follow them may become partakers of the judgment that awaits them.

The Bible's stand on false prophets is clear. Apart from the abovementioned points, the Bible teaches us to understand their nature and motive. A little search through God's Word effortlessly reveals God's mind concerning these wolves in sheep's skin.

The Bible clarifies that they serve their belly and not the true God. They serve their own pockets rather than having a genuine interest in populating the kingdom of God by depopulating the kingdom of Satan.

Philippians 3 tells us some interesting facts about these false prophets, otherwise known as enemies of the Cross. They may even wear the crucifix on their necks all day, but their conduct opposes its message. *Verses 18 and 19* show that they mind earthly things; their God is their belly, and what they glory in shall be their shame. They delight in material wealth and their ability to fool innocent Christians. That which they rejoice in shall bring them shame. *Romans 16:18* also emphasizes the above.

The stand of the Bible on the false prophets who serve as leaders in Christianity includes their comparison to 'whited sepulchers.' Matthew 23 speaks of the scribes and Pharisees who bear great semblance to the present-day false prophets, false preachers, and false leaders of Christianity today.

Among other qualifications and accusations of these despicable characters, in *verse 27,* Jesus described *these men as being like whited sepulchers who appear to be beautiful outwardly but are full of the dead bones of many they have misled into their destructions*. He also describes them as full of uncleanness; in *verse 13*, Jesus says *they stand in the way; they neither go in nor allow their ignorant followers to go in. They neither enter into the door to the grace provided by Christ Jesus, yet they fool their followers into ignoring this door that leads to life.*

One other interesting symbolic representation of these false prophets in the Bible is in *Jeremiah 2:13 (KJV): For my people have committed two evils; they have forsaken me the fountain of living waters, and hewed them out cisterns, broken cisterns, that can hold no water.*

The Bible refers to these false prophets who arrogate to themselves the status of God in the lives of their followers as 'broken cisterns.' They are neither natural fountain of life like the true God (Psalms 36:9a), neither are they wells of water but are faulty cisterns built by men that cannot hold water.

Jeremiah 2:13 contains an in-depth analysis of false prophets or false human gods. A cistern depends on water from rain which comes from God, or water from men fetched from other sources, also coming from God. These human gods survive on God's grace but portray themselves as gods among men. To make matters worse, they are 'broken' and unable to hold the grace made available. Yet, some spiritually insensitive Christians run to these gods for safety, rejecting the only true God, albeit unknowingly.

Unfortunately, the evils done by false prophets and false preachers primarily go unchecked. Many mushroom churches spring up mostly in areas populated by desperate and poor people to fool ignorant and despairing Christians. In third-world countries, the quest for miracles and material wealth has ensnared many believers and caused many to fall prey to the hands of false prophets and chase after idols and false gods.

Many of these fake men of God emphasized money paid into the coffers of the church or pastors rather than holiness and a decent walk with God. Shamelessly, they tailor their sermons towards prosperity preaching and may link every topic treated back to the pursuit of prosperity and a need to bring more money to the church to qualify for God'sblessings. There have been cases of these so-called men of God praying death over individuals who fail to pay their tithes or offerings or sow a seed. Many of them flash their wealth and exploit members, coaxing them to believe that only a person who sows to the church attracts such wealth, and to access such "GRACE," as they call it, is to GIVE, not to God but THEM.

Some of these false men of God who claim to be prophets go as far as giving scary prophesies to their prey to con them of their money. They are prophets of doom who only see calamities rather than blessings. By putting fear in the minds of ignorant Christians of little faith, they build control over them for selfish aims. They have destroyed so many homes and lives cut short, and so many lives rubbished by these false prophecies. A few years ago, a single woman over 30 years old was told by a false prophet that her mom was behind her singleness. He insisted that her mother was a witch determined to destroy her life. The woman's relationship with her mom was damaged from that moment.

A so-called man of God assured an entrepreneur that his business was failing because his beloved wife was using juju on him and had bottled his destiny; shortly after, he divorced his wife but not before inflicting physical and verbal torture.

Stories abound of toddlers marked as witches and killed or left for dead, or prophecies of death to exploit Christians. Many have been left handicapped in their minds by these men of God. The Bible clearly says in Matthew 24:11-13 that many

FALSE PROPHETS WILL RISE.

"...and many false prophets will arise and mislead many. Because of the multiplication of wickedness, the love of most will grow cold. But the one who perseveres to the end will be saved...."

Sadly, because many LAZY BELIEVERS choose not to know God for themselves, it is easy to fall prey to these so-called Men of God.

2 Timothy 4:3 (AMP) puts it beautifully, *"For the time will come when people will not tolerate sound doctrine and accurate instruction [that challenges them with God's truth]; but wanting to have their ears tickled [with something pleasing], they will accumulate for themselves [many]teachers [one after another, chosen] to satisfy their own desires and to support the errors they hold,"*

The Message version says it in a way that hits close to home, *"You're going to find that there will be times when people will have no stomach for solid teaching, but will fill up on spiritual junk food—catchy opinions that tickle their fancy. They'll turn their backs on truth and chase mirages. But you—keep your eye on what you're doing; accept the hard times along with the good; keep the Message alive; do a thorough job as God's servant."*

"Keep your eye on what you're doing; accept the hard times along with the good." Because people do not want to continuously experience downtimes and be fed with milk, they are always searching for words and prophecy that tickle

their lusts and desires—self-seeking prayers and fasting to feed their earthly lusts and covetousness.

The control of the false prophets often consumes their victims that some of them place pictures of their prophets in their houses for protection, while the prophets go everywhere with a convoy of security men. It is unfortunate to see Christians adorn their cars and homes with stickers of their false prophet leaders for safety. In contrast, the leaders only go out in armored vehicles with a heavy security presence around them.

Many Christians have left the faith and no longer have a relationship with God. Many budding Christians have unknowingly followed these false preachers and engaged in faulty doctrines, rituals, services, or worship. Many have unwittingly offered strange fire on the altar, following in the footsteps of their trusted fathers in the Lord.

Also, many preys of these false men of God realize their errors, and rather than leave just the church or the scheming men of God; they leave the body of Christ. Such poor victims end up throwing away their salvation.

Some victims of false prophets who break away from their bondage resort to alternative means of seeking help like sorcery and voodoo. By submitting to such lesser gods, they miss their salvation and are lost to the kingdom of Satan. In other words, even when they break away from the false prophets, the residual effects of their experience still trail them and lead them to hell. Only a timely intervention by God and prayers of the saints can save such people.

Many Christians have missed their destinies and couldn't fulfill their calling because of false prophets and schemes. They, especially young adults, have been conned out of their original purpose by the 'lying hollow tongues of the serpents' mimicking sheep. Stories abound of people who were told their destiny did not lie in the path of education. Some were made to believe certain professions they love will not fetch them the blessed life they desire.

Such victims of false prophesy act based on such prophesies and end up causing their destinies irreparable damages. Some fail to go to school and find it difficult retracing their steps say, after several children. Some marry wrongly and regret it for life even after they find Christ, the church will never support a divorce on such grounds. They are coaxed into marrying the wrong person because a man or woman's name was used in a spiritual lottery on their behalf and disguised as God's plan.

Some false prophets have failed to question the source of the money of some of their wealthy members who support them financially. Rather than find out how these members make their money, they pray for them to make more money from their 'business.' As a result, such persons no longer feel remorse. They find confidence in the indirect support of their fake prophet leaders. The apparent end of such men is destruction and eternal damnation.

Many young Christians, who seek after false prophets, have been fooled into believing their mother or father to be their enemy. The same mother, who did not kill them from childhood, suddenly earned the witch's tag from a false prophet and promptly lost the relationship between mother and child. This is more common among Afro-Asians, where some communities still believe in stoning a witch or an assumed witch to death. Even innocent old women who earn the tag of a 'witch' from a false prophet can be stoned to death without anyone asking questions or further investigation.

Worse still, many homes have been destroyed and family dreams and ambitions shattered by the lying tongues of false prophets. When unsuspecting Christians believe their spouses are their enemies, it can only lead to a shaky home structure. In many such cases, the home eventually breaks with a separation of the spouses. The magnitude of such ungodly development is better understood by considering the emotional trauma it can cause to the people involved. While both husband and wife are affected, the children from the marriage are the worst hit. Yet the lying prophets fail to consider those little ones when spinning their evil lies.

One unfortunate effect of the activities of false prophets is the shame it brings to the body of Christ. Unbelievers hear of the activities of false prophets and generalize their actions as part of Christian doctrine. When evangelists go out to win the souls of such unbelievers, they readily point to the works of the false prophets as a fault in Christianity.

Also, some young and aspiring believers who hear the deeds of these supposed men of God are discouraged. Many of them draw back, while others slow down their church commitment. The secondary effects of the activities of false prophets are often not attached to the actions of the false prophets, no thanks to the level of ignorance in our societies about such evil acts.

Many experiences abound about the unfortunate effects of false prophets on Christianity and the church. A false prophet once told his members the world was ending in 2000. He then encouraged them to sell their properties and bring the money to the church. The members did as directed by their pastor, and all eagerly awaited the set date. The date came, and there was heavy rain; there were thunderclaps accompanied by flashing lightning, but the voice of God was not in any of them.

The rain stopped, yet there was no rapture or anything like it. The following day speedily arrived, with the world not showing any interest in ending. The next day came and sped by too. After several days, some members began to doubt the sweet tongue of their pastor. Eventually, it dawned on the church members that they had fallen prey to a major scam.

A false prophet told a man that his wife was a witch. He began to pick quarrels with the innocent woman, which later resulted in beating. His prophet's hollow tongue pushed him into another woman's arms. Before long, he abandoned his family and spent all day with the second woman. After several years with the second woman, he suffered a stroke and was surprised when the second woman ran away from him. His first woman picked him up and took him to her abode, where they live together until now but without the spark and glow that existed in their relationship. The children wanted nothing to do with their prodigal father, who had wasted all his wealth on the strange woman he met in his false prophet's church.

Another example of the damaging effect of the hollow tongue of a false prophet on Christians is the case of a beautiful young lady. Many desired her, but unfortunately, she refused the overtures of all the young men around her because of a prophecy she was given. According to her, a prophet told her she would marry a professor, so she waited until she was on the brink of menopause before marrying the only person available to her. Today she is almost fifty and yet without a child. Her realization that the prophecy she rested her faith on was fake could not reverse the damage done to her destiny.

Similar tales abound in churches across Christian sects of false prophets who set people on the path of destruction or irreparable damage. Such false prophets may pay for their wrongs, but their prey may not be able to come out of the damage done to them by these false prophets.

Surprisingly, some Christians still go to them for help even when negative testimonies trail certain false prophets. There are several reasons for this ranging from the ridiculous to the unfortunate.

Some Christians seek help from such broken cisterns out of pure ignorance. They are oblivious that even an angel of darkness can camouflage as an angel of light. They go after aesthetics rather than the real thing. They judge by what they see rather than what the Holy Spirit says.

Some run after the serpents in disguise because they lack a discerning spirit *1 Cor 2:14 states that a spiritual man judges or discerns all things, but he is rightly judged or discerned by any man.* It takes a man with the Spirit of God to discern the things that pertain to the Spirit of God.

Some Christians get lured into patronizing false prophets by friends and family. They forget that the Bible admonishes that whatever part of your body or life makes you miss heaven should be cut off. This includes family and friends.

Several Christians willingly deliver themselves into the nets of these false prophets because of impatience. When trials and temptation come their way, and they feel God is not responding fast enough, they seek an alternative source of help. And like Saul and the witch of Endor, their end is always bad. Their situation is worse as they once had their salvation but threw it away because of the trials of life.

Jeremiah 2:11 (KJV) says: Hath a nation changed their gods, which are yet no gods? But my people have changed their glory for that which doth not profit.

The negative results of seeking the help of false prophets are numerous, but all eventually lead to loss of salvation if the one seeking such prophets fails to repent.

Many lose the bond of unity in their homes because they believe in a lying prophet. Some get separated from their parents because they put their confidence in a broken cistern. Some have died, taking risks based on the assurance given to them by false prophets. These and more are the outcome of trusting in a false prophet rather than a true prophet of God.

However, the good news is that even the false prophets are mere storms of life. They are agents of temptations led by the devil to torment his targets. The succor of a true child of God then lies in *1 Cor 10:13*. *It clearly states that no temptation could overcome a true child of God, as God will always create a way out for His own.*

Therefore, every child of God who finds himself entangled in the web of a false prophet could take solace in the Word of God. The Word of God can open the closed eyes and destinies of those dead or dying to the things of the Spirit of God.

Another approach to completely breaking out of the spell of the false prophet is deliverance or intense prayer. This could be necessary as some demons might have been released into the lives of the prey by the false prophets.

Confession is vital, whatever approach is taken to break a prey of a false prophet free from his predicament. Such a person must be willing to accept his fault and seek forgiveness and restoration.

James 5:16 (KJV): Confess your faults one to another and pray one for another, that ye may be healed. The effectual fervent prayer of a righteous man availeth much.

Unfortunately, many faithful children of God still do not know how to identify a false prophet. They relate with them, trust them, and lean on them until they are sucked into the 'whited sepulcher' of the false prophets.

Chapter Two

Bearers of the Fruits of Deceits

Beware of false prophets, which come to you in sheep's clothing, but inwardly they are ravening wolves. Ye shall know them by their fruits. Do men gather grapes of thorns or figs of thistles? Even so, every good tree bringeth forth good fruit, but a corrupt tree bringeth forth evil fruit. A good tree cannot bring forth evil fruit, and neither can a corrupt tree bring forth good fruit. Every tree that bringeth not forth good fruit is hewn down and cast into the fire. Wherefore by their fruits ye shall know them. Matthew 7: 15-20 (KJV).

The Bible has a lot to say about false prophets or false preachers. In the excerpt above, Jesus Christ expressly spoke about false prophets, giving us a clear idea of who they are. We can see they are considered pretenders who seek to portray themselves as what they are not. *2 Corinthians 11:14-15 (KJV) states: And no marvel; for Satan himself is transformed into an angel of light.*

Therefore, it is no remarkable thing if His ministers also are transformed into the ministers of righteousness, whose end shall be according to their works. They pretend to be white sheep when they are wolves. They pretend to be of the light when they are agents of darkness. Their ends shall be according to their works.

Jesus Christ pointed out many years ago that we should be conscious of their fruits; we should take note of the fruits of their lips and deeds, and we shall be able to discern who they are. He further compared them to a corrupt tree bearing evil fruits. I pray for you today; you shall not fall prey to these unscrupulous agents in Jesus' name.

Who or what are these false prophets? They are people, either men or women, who profess to speak the mind of God but only carry out agendas different from His will. Some of them only speak out of their personal agenda, bothering on greed for worldly riches, power, or influence, while some unwittingly carry out the agenda of their devil father, the father of all lies. They are whited sepulchers guiding the soul of the innocent to the grave rather than pointing them to the way that breeds life, that is, Jesus Christ (John 14:6).

Mysteriously enough, some false prophets are not even aware that they are operating under other powers rather than that of the only true God. They yield to the influence of certain "fathers in the Lord," who dictate all they do in relating with their ignorant victims.

Such false prophets are the worst of the lot as they are not even aware that they are evil conduits conveying the souls of the innocent to hell.

A good example is the case of many modern-day Christians who unknowingly worship some so-called men of God because of the wonders they perform, not knowing these 'men of God' use diabolical means to perform wonders, arranged miracles, and testimonies. They will argue and even stake their lives to defend these false prophets, judging only by what they see with their eyes and not by the Spirit of God. When such Christians rise to become ministers under such false prophets, they innocently encourage other innocent people to come into the same boat of destruction, conveying their souls to hell. Such men, either ignorant or not, are also false prophets and preachers.

There are different classes of false prophets. They can be classified in diverse ways, along other lines and yardsticks. The classification below is only intended to understand better who or what these agents of Satan are.

- » **Scammers after money:** These ones engage in this nefarious act to fill their belly.

For they that are such serve not our Lord Jesus Christ, but their own belly; and by good words and fair speeches deceive the hearts of the simple. Romans 16:18 (KJV).

They use the altar to serve their belly rather than Christ. They use sweet words to deceive people to con them into parting with their money. Their end is destruction.

Meats for the belly, and the belly for meats: but God shall destroy both it and them. Now the body is not for fornication, but for the Lord, and the Lord for the body. 1 Corinthians 6:13a (KJV).

> » **The deluded:** These false prophets can be said to have zeal without knowledge of God. They have not met God; they are not receiving from Him, yet are deluded, thinking they preach and prophesy according to the will of God. It may sound strange, but it is not new, as prophet Jeremiah prophesied about such prophets.

Then the LORD said unto me, The prophets prophesy lies in my name: I sent them not, neither have I commanded them, neither spake unto them: they prophesy unto you a false vision and divination, and a thing of naught, and the delusion of their heart. Jeremiah 14:14 (KJV).

Some deluded prophets may be suffering from psychological or psychiatric disturbances unknown to them. They claim to hear voices and do things based on what they believe. Unfortunately, their sincerity would count for nothing, and their followers will not be guiltless before God, as they have failed to see that these are false prophets.

» **The sincere-gone-wrong false prophets:** Some false prophets or preachers had the calling, heeded the call, and started their race well. Along the line, issues of life caused them to go wrong. Like Adam in the garden of Eden, they start well, but along the line, ate of the forbidden fruit and are lost. Many find it difficult to retrace their steps because of shame and other reasons. Some started well but soon gave room to envy and jealousy when they saw other prophets or preachers doing better.

Some indeed preach Christ even of envy and strife, and some also of goodwill: The one preach Christ of contention, not sincerely, supposing to add affliction to my bonds. Philippians 1:15-16 (KJV).

Some started well but fell into sin and refused to confess and forsake their sins. They continue to preach, but the Lord's Spirit no longer recognizes them. They forgot that a successful walk with God is not necessarily in not falling at all, but in rising each time, you fall. Slipping into sin or falling does not mean a man will automatically be alienated from God. Still, unwillingness to rise after a fall or to repent after sin creates the barrier between man and God.

For a just man falleth seven times, and riseth up again: but the wicked shall fall into mischief. Proverbs 24:16 (KJV).

Such false prophets share something in common with Satan himself. *Ezekiel 28:15 (KJV) Says: Thou wast perfect in thy ways from the day that thou wast created, till iniquity was found in thee.* Although the verse refers to Satan, the report fits many good-gone-bad prophets and preachers.

» **Eager to impress false prophets:** These are prophets who hear from God but soon lose it- out of their eagerness to impress men. When the Lord says one thing, they report three. When a genuine revelation comes from God, they blow it into enormous proportions to impress people. *Romans 11:29 (KJV) says; For the gifts and calling of God are without repentance.* God will persevere with them for a season, but a time comes when He will cease to reckon with them, and their gift will remain latent in them. Such false men of God then use their five senses and experience to prophesy and preach. Unless they repent from their over-zealous ways aimed at pleasing the high and mighty in the society, they shall in no wise perish like other false prophets.

» **The self-called false prophets** are prophets or preachers who did not hear the call to the office from the Holy Spirit. They want to become a prophet and decide to assume the role of one without the calling or backing of the Holy Spirit.

Not every one that saith unto me, Lord, Lord, shall enter into the kingdom of heaven; but he that doeth the will of my Father which is in heaven. Many will say to me in that day, Lord, Lord, have we not prophesied in thy name? and in thy name have cast out devils? And in thy name done many wonderful works? And then will I profess unto them, I never knew you: depart from me, ye that work iniquity. Matthew 7:21-23 (KJV).

The verse suggests that some so-called prophets may even perform miracles in the name of Christ but may not be recognized by Christ. There are several reasons why this is possible. One of such reasons is that when a prophet or preacher speaks and prays in the name of Christ Jesus, even if he is not recognized by Jesus Christ, the faith of his hearers may yet deliver them. The fact that his hearers experience a miracle does not mean that the prophet or preacher has a right standing with God. To make matters worse, such preachers begin to believe the miracles have to do with them, and it even causes some of them to brag about such miracles, further compounding their miseries.

Another way this sort of calamity happens to some so-called prophets of God is lasciviousness. Many who are called to be ushers would rather be choristers because they feel choristers are seen and better appreciated by the congregation. Some people called into counseling want to be prophets for self-glory, while others called into managing church funds opt to be pastors because they see the money flowing into the church.

Such men are like a farmer who plants his precious seeds on another man's farm; when harvest time comes, he shall discover late that he has wasted his seeds.

They have only called themselves, and their works are not recognized. Neither can such perform optimally in the areas they have assigned themselves. No matter how big a spoon is, it cannot make a good hammer. No matter how sharp a screwdriver can be, it can never effectively carry out the work of a knife. Stay in the calling to which God has called you so that you do not become a false prophet unwittingly.

» **The initiated false prophets:** Some false prophets were unknowingly initiated into falsehood, and they refuse to come out of that falsehood. Some, under the sect they belong to or the people they relate with, got initiated into diabolical cults, like the diabolical false prophets they associate with. Some even get initiated willingly. *In Acts 18,* a certain Simon the sorcerer approached them when he heard the apostles' preaching and offered them money for the gift of working miracles. If the apostles had wrought the miracles out of diabolical means, he would have been automatically initiated. Many people today willingly give money to so-called men of God to impart the gift of healing to them. If it is gotten by money, then it is not of God. *Matthew 10:8 (KJV) says: Heal the sick, cleanse the lepers, raise the dead, cast out devils: freely ye have received, freely give.*

» **False prophet by compulsion:** This is a new trend in Christianity today. You see a genuine man of God with a thriving ministry insisting that his son or wife inherits the headship of the church. The person forced to inherit the role may not even have the calling; the result is the fall of such ministry. Cases like that abound in the body of Christ today. It is always sad when such churches fade into oblivion and begin to live on past glory. Their members always say things like, "When papa was still alive..." Or "If papa were to be alive...".

Another form of such falsehood on the altar is falsehood emanating from marriage. A woman married to a pastor is pressured to live up to the congregation's expectations. Even if her calling is children's ministry or keeping of sanctuary, she finds herself thrust into the spotlight by her husband and the congregation. Many of such women fall into the error of giving false declarations and prophecies to please men. The end again is destruction.

False prophets can, however, be identified by their characteristics. According to Thomas Brooks (1806-1880), a man well-loved by the popular C H Spurgeon, *there are seven characteristics of false preachers and teachers:*

1. **They are men-pleasers***: Galatians 1:10 (KJV) says: For do I now persuade men or God? or do I seek to please men? for if I yet pleased men, I should not be the servant of Christ.* These preachers or prophets speak to please the ears rather than profit the heart. *Isaiah 30:10* makes it clear that some men influence the prophet to prophesy what they want to hear. *Jeremiah 5:31* refers to this as a horrible thing in the land.

2. False preachers throw dirt at God's people. False preachers are notable for casting dirt, scorn, and reproach on the persons, names, and credits of Christ's most faithful ambassadors. He identified Korah,

Dathan, and Abiram as examples of false preachers who cast aspersion on Moses. The result is they were swallowed alive by the ground.

3. False preachers are driven by their hearts and heads. *Jeremiah 23:16 (KJV) says Thus saith the LORD of hosts, Hearken not unto the words of the prophets that prophesy unto you: they make you vain: they speak a vision of their own heart, and not out of the mouth of the LORD.* Aren't there many Christians whose visions are but golden delusion, lying vanities, and brain-sick fantasies? According to Thomas Brooks, these are Satan's great benefactors, such as divine justice will hang up in hell as the greatest malefactors if the Physician of souls does not prevent it.

4. False preachers pass over the law and the gospel for other things. False preachers quickly pass over the great and weighty things of the law and the gospel and stand most upon those things that are of minor importance and concernment to the souls of men.

5. False preachers use clever language and appearances to disguise themselves. They cover their dangerous principles with very fair speeches and plausible pretenses, with high notions and golden expressions. *2 Corinthians 11:13 (KJV) states: For such are false apostles, deceitful workers, transforming themselves into the apostles of Christ.*

6. False teachers try to win people to their opinion by

winning debates. They strive to win at arguments more than to make people better through their conversations. *Matthew 23:15 (KJV) says, "Woe unto you, scribes and Pharisees, hypocrites! for ye compass sea and land to make one proselyte, and when he is made, ye make him twofold more the child of hell than yourselves.* They busy themselves with long speeches to impress men and win them to themselves rather than God.

7. False preachers seek to gain from their followers. They always look for ways of making merchandise of their followers. *2 Peter 2:1-3 (KJV) explains thus: But there were false prophets also among the people, even as there shall be false teachers among you, who privily shall bring in damnable heresies, even denying the Lord that bought them, and bring upon themselves swift destruction. And many shall follow their pernicious ways; by reason of whom, the way of truth shall be evil spoken of. And through covetousness shall they with feigned words make merchandise of you: whose judgment now of a long time lingereth not, and their damnation slumbereth not.*

They eye your goods more than your GOOD and care about servicing themselves rather than the souls of their followers. They long to have your substance and care, not if Satan had your soul. Today, many false prophets openly display their falsehood, yet they go unchecked by the necessary authorities. Unfortunately, the regions with the most open willingness to accept Jesus Christ are affected most. The Bible has made it clear that these agents of darkness, though disguised as angels of light, but by their fruits, we shall know them. A famous prophet, who openly said during a sermon on a Sunday that he paid quality money to a man of God to get the impartation of the power to heal, must remain a suspect until proven otherwise. The gift of God cannot be bought with money, and no true man of God will accept money to impart the power to heal.

A popular man of God from a famous African country, who instructed his followers to eat grass like goats, should not claim to be a true man of God. He also urged them to take bleaching agents and detergents for healing. At the very least, these are not of God. Preachers who preach the word of God to perfection but do not live by what they preach are not worthy to be called true preachers or prophets. A man who preaches against adultery and fornication but has a secret second wife is already a candidate for hell while on earth. He is not worthy of being called a man of God. Another terrible trend among these agents of darkness among the children of light is the staging of miracles. Many false prophets arrange for people to fake miracles, and you see them jumping and jubilating, attributing the effort to themselves rather than God. God does not require any man to stage miracles for His glory, and such false prophets shall have their place in hell.

Some false prophets, who have little understanding of using the pulpit and altar, now invite famous comedians to church to attract the crowd. They turn the house of God into a place of frivolous entertainment. They make a mockery of the sacredness of the pulpit. The pulpit is meant for pulling men out of the pit, not for putting men in the pit. Unfortunately, by their antics, these false prophets end up using the pulpit to destroy rather than liberate many.

A false prophet who engages in occultic and fetish practice for powers has thrown his soul into the lake of fire. The stand of the Word of God remains firm, an*d 2 Corinthians 6:14 (KJV) elaborates it well: Be ye not unequally yoked together with unbelievers: for what fellowship hath righteousness with unrighteousness? and what communion hath light with darkness?*

Every such counterfeit prophet shall have their place in the lake of fire. Some false prophets and preachers gain popularity through their ability to speak fluently and make people pay attention. As a result, they meet and relate with the high and mighty in society; there was a case, for instance, of a prominent pastor from a famous African country whose private jet was used by a cabal to purchase ammunition from another country. When the judgment of God shall come, their popularity and societal influence shall count for nothing. One thing is sure, their place in hell shall not be given to another.

Another avenue to worldly greatness and wealth of some of these false men of God is through occultic associations. A famous man of God who headed the Christian association in his country and used to be very vibrant in his youth now appears in public in all black apparel with dark shades and several funny rings on his fingers. He also does not criticize the government anymore but instead rolls with the top politicians of his country. Some time ago, there was a story in the news about his wife going to the market in a chauffeur-driven limousine. The affluence and influence of their family cannot but be noticed, and the stories making rounds about the pastor's occultic activities cannot also be easily swept under the carpet. Whether those stories are true or not, whether the observers see right or not, when the judgment of God shall come, all shall be made known.

Many false prophets fail to change, even when confronted with overwhelming truth about their stand with God. Their usual is to spin up some cocoon of mystery, claiming people are too mortal to understand the relationship between them and God. Some get angry and lay curses on those who dare to confront them. Even the Bible recognizes that certain people are destined for destruction, and such false prophets are in this category if they fail to repent.

Finally, a tree can hardly hide its fruits for long, just as a man cannot hide his true character forever. False prophets and preachers abound around us, but we shall know them by their fruits. I pray that God will open your eyes to see the true nature of the men of God around you in Jesus' name.

Chapter Three

Occultic Influence in the Church.

Ye shall keep my sabbaths, and reverence my sanctuary: I am the LORD. Regard not them that have familiar spirits, neither seek after wizards, to be defiled by them: I am the LORD your God. Leviticus 19:20-31 (KJV)

Occultism refers to knowledge of a mysterious realm, which has to do with hidden things shrouded in darkness. There are many of their practices associated with occultism, including rituals and bizarre rules for daily living.

The father of darkness and everything of darkness is Satan. Hence, it is safe to say occultism is of the devil. We can say occultic practices are activities done by men, leveraging mysterious powers and beliefs outside of Jesus Christ.

Many traditional beliefs accommodate knowledge and practices steeped in hidden darkness and some religions. Some Christian sects also make the mistake of handling mysteries with levity. While we admit that mysteries abound in Christianity and Christian practice, we should never be ignorant of the devil's devices. A genuine Christian must be sure of the origin of the voice he hears leading him into mysterious practices or beliefs.

Isaiah 30:21 (KJV) says: And thine ears shall hear a word behind thee, saying, This is the way, walk ye in it, when ye turn to the right hand, and when ye turn to the left.

But you, as a spiritual man, must learn to discern and test every spirit. While there will be contact with the supernatural, while our lives must experience mysterious occurrences whether we are Christians or not, it remains that it is not always the hand of God that does the first touch. Not every mysterious voice you hear is the voice of God.

Every action or decision you are led to make must be sifted

on the altar of the word of God. No matter how sweet or innocent or needed it may be, if it does not agree with the word of God, then it is not of God.

If a mysterious voice, either in your head or through someone, is telling you to go and kill an innocent man to make money, you do not need your pastor to say it is not the voice of God. That must be the devil at work.

The evil instruction from the pit of hell may be subtle and innocuous. For instance, when an inner voice instructs you to pay back evil for an evil deed done to you; or not to call an erring brother to order. If the word of God cannot explain such instruction, if such action opposes the will of God for you as a child of God, then such voice or instruction is not of God.

Many people listening to mysterious voices have destroyed their destinies in the name of listening to mysterious voices. In the name of believing in the teachings of prophets from churches who have a deep belief in the mysterious have been misled and fallen into deep pits from which they cannot climb out.

Occultism and the church
In some churches with no leaders with a sound understanding of the word of God, issues that cannot be explained are quickly classified as mysterious or spiritual. The eagerness of some Christians to have a supernatural experience has also driven many into classifying natural occurrences as mysterious.

For example, water dripping from the feet of the statue of

Christ in a church was quickly termed mysterious, and the water miraculous. Some even claimed to have experienced miracles from drinking the water. Later, it was discovered that the water was draining from a broken faucet in a nearby toilet. It resulted from a fault in a plumbing system and is not necessarily a mystery.

Another case is a giant owl that flew into a large auditorium of Christians and was promptly killed and tagged evil. While it may be an evil bird, we know that a bird flying from outer darkness may be attracted by light; once inside the brightly lit hall, it may become blinded and confused.

We are not shying away from the fact that Christianity as a way of life is an embodiment of mysteries. From the birth of Christ to his death and ascension, to the sending of the Holy Spirit and the impartations of the gifts of the spirit, these and more are deeply mysterious.

The line between Christian mystery and occultism is not so thin for a child of God with a discerning spirit. *1 Corinthians 2:15 (KJV) But he that is spiritual judgeth all things, yet he himself is judged of no man.*

Christian mysteries are backed by the word of God, while occultism has no place in Christ Jesus.

However, many false prophets have found comfort in using occultism to fool people into becoming their victims. When their awkward activities are questioned, they claim it is a thing of mystery. Some will even say it is beyond human understanding and should be accepted without question.

Broken cisterns, leading men to destruction! Even the Bible encourages that we test every spirit, but they prefer that their evil acts be accepted without question.

Some of them carry out occultic activities in ignorance, being led by the devil but believing God is leading them.

For God is not the author of confusion, but of peace, as in all churches of the saints. 1 Corinthians 14:33 (KJV).

Accepting some questionable acts by false prophets in the first church as prophetic mysteries has paved the way for false prophets to go even deeper into occultism. They influence the church both physically and spiritually through the power of occultism. They claim to see visions and know the future through the gift of the Spirit of God while they lean on the shoulders of demonic masters directing their every action and giving them revelations.

Interestingly, such revelations may even happen, but they do not necessarily make them mouthpieces of God. Their actions and revelations, no matter how vivid they may be, if not of God, are not of God.

The Bible refers to them as rebellious children. They rebel against God while doing things contrary to the will of God while still holding unto His name as His children. According to Prophet Samuel in *1 Samuel 15:23a (KJV)*, which says: *"For rebellion is as the sin of witchcraft, and stubbornness is as iniquity and idolatry."* We can easily see the proximity of such rebellious children in the practice of witchcraft.

Furthermore, in *Isaiah 30:1 (KJV)*, the prophet declares thus: *Woe to the rebellious children, saith the LORD, that take counsel, but not of me; and that cover with a covering, but not of my spirit, that they may add sin to sin.*

According to the text above, these false prophets take counsel, advice, and instructions not from God but from the devil. Their protection from being discovered as counterfeit men of God is also not of God nor His spirit. The result of their line of actions is that they add sin to sin.

How are they adding sin to sin? *Jeremiah 2:13 (KJV)* explains, *For my people have committed two evils; they have forsaken me the fountain of living waters, and hewed them out cisterns, broken cisterns, that can hold no water.*

Knowing God and not acknowledging Him is a sin for a so-called rebellious Christian. Seeking covering and help or power from other means is an added sin. They indeed add sin to sin.

Isaiah 30:2 (KJV) continues from chapter one, saying: *That walk to go down into Egypt, and have not asked at my mouth; to strengthen themselves in the strength of Pharaoh, and to trust in the shadow of Egypt!*

These rebellious false prophets go after alternative power sources without hearing from God. They strengthen themselves in the power of the occultic and trust in their demonic masters. In *Isaiah 30:3 (KJV)*, we see their expected end: *Therefore, shall the strength of Pharaoh be your shame, and the trust in the shadow of Egypt your confusion.* The power they rely on will eventually fail them and bring them down to the mire of shame. A day will come when their faces shall be covered in confusion when the demons they converse with and rely so much on shall fail them. Satan is determined to do all he can to destroy the church. One of his weapons in this present time is occultism. He is fast influencing the church's affairs with occultic practices and manifestations, many of which go unnoticed.

Be sober, be vigilant; because your adversary the devil, as a roaring lion, walketh about, seeking whom he may devour. 1 Peter 5:8 (KJV).

The struggle between the church of God and Satan is not a minor skirmish or brawl but a full-scale war transcending the physical to the spiritual. It is a continuous war with no break whatsoever. That is why it is said that a man's mind is a constant battleground of choices and decisions. This war is one against enemies that are well trained and organized. Their purpose is clear to them, destruction of the Christian faith. They do not entertain sentiments regarding the work their master has sent them to do. The more reason the fallen angels turned into demons and are so dangerous. They should, however, not be feared by any true child of God, for the grace to overcome them lies in us.

Ye are of God, little children, and have overcome them: because greater is he that is in you than he that is in the world. 1 John 4:4 (KJV).

False prophets are essential tools in the hand of the devil

in his fight against the church of God. Once the devil gets these false prophets to do his bidding, he uses them as insider attacking agents against the body of Christ.

Some ways through which the devil is fighting the church using occultic means include the following, among others:

1. Temptation, Deceit, and Deception: The devil does not have a new tactic. He keeps recycling his old tactics, yet some ignorant men still fall into his nets. He tempts with wealth, power, and popularity. Unfortunately, many children of God are still slipping into the trap. He uses deceit in clothing occultic activities on Christian garb. For instance, he makes the worship of statues and past heroes of faith look normal, contrary to the Bible. The same trick of deceit and deception caused Adam and Eve to fall out of favor with The Almighty God. Damage that all men suffer from till this present day.

   Lest Satan should get an advantage of us: for we are not ignorant of his devices. 2 Corinthians 2:11 (KJV)

2. Enticement in the form of miracles and wonders: The devil empowers his agents, the false prophets, to perform miracles and teach heresies in churches. Many people are deaf to the heretic details of their preaching and are focused on the wonders they perform. They feel it does not matter when a so-called prophet of God is not sound in the Word of God if he prophesies and sees visions; this is deception at its peak! You cannot be a representative of someone you do not know and who

does not reckon with you. Even when these prophets say things contrary to Bible teaching, they brush it aside, claiming it is because he is not educated or due to a slip of the tongue; blind men being led by the blind!

But every man is tempted, when he is drawn away of his own lust, and enticed. Then when lust hath conceived, it bringeth forth sin: and sin, when it is finished, bringeth forth death. Do not err, my beloved brethren. James 1:14-16 (KJV).

Lust draws many present-day Christians into searching for miracles, signs, and wonders, allowing them to be enticed into ungodliness by satanic agents. This leads to sin, which results in spiritual death.

3. The increased divorce rate in churches: It is now commonplace to hear of broken marriages with some reference to the involvement of a so-called man of God. A man who is supposed to be an elder in a church had a running issue with his wife over infidelity, and eventually, the pastor of the church was involved, of course. Rather than condemn the man's action for having affairs with other women, the pastor threatened the woman with a piece of divorce advice to her husband. He told her, "You should be glad he has not married one of the women." The man's wife became depressed for days, and it took the grace of God and the support of her loved ones to get her out of the depression. The devil is attacking marriages, and false prophets are at the forefront of his agenda. They have

become battering rams with which the devil is bashing the bonds in some Christian homes into smithereens.

Many cases abound where prophets tell people they have married wrongly. They tell people, mostly men, that the women they are married to are not their wives. It creates bad blood in the homes and, ultimately, extramarital affairs on the part of the man. Sometimes, the woman pays back the man in his coin, and the home soon becomes a shadow of what it used to be. Very few marriages manage to return to what they used to be after going this far. *Neither gives place to the devil. Ephesians 4:27 (KJV)*

Once marriages suffer within the church, then the church herself suffers. If more people in the church are going to hell, the church as the bride of Christ cannot be seen as a good mother. Many good men in church have resorted to drinking and some womanizing just because a lacuna was created in their lives by the absence of a woman. This may be a result of divorce or death. The church needs to rise to protect threatened homes. The better the homes of families in church are protected, the more the church herself is preserved.

4. Sucking more innocent Christians into Occultic bondages: Another strategy of the devil against the church is making occultism look attractive and harmless. It is no longer news that more churches and men of God now use aids in place of faith in ministrations. From anointing oil to the handkerchief, widely called the

mantle, to water and wine. These items are acceptable in Christianity. But the trend in which some prophets request strange things like feces, animals, or the bedspread of their victims is unacceptable. Some of these wicked prophets even ask for the sand of the footprint of the enemy of their clients. These false prophets deceive many innocent Christians causing them to become blind to the glorious gospel of Jesus Christ. *But if our gospel be hid, it is hid to them that are lost: In whom the God of this world hath blinded the minds of them which believe not, lest the light of the glorious gospel of Christ, who is the image of God, should shine unto them. 2 Corinthians 4:3-4 (KJV).*

5. Another occultic strategy of the devil is to confuse the church by instigating fights among men of God. When reputable men of God are lured into in-fighting, a lacuna is created in the hearts of their followers through which the demon of weariness and disbursement can go in. The Bible encourages decency and orderliness in the church, but we cannot shy away from the fact that we still experience cold wars between parties within the same church. It is a plan of the devil. *Let all things be done decently and in order. 1 Corinthians 14:40 (KJV).*

6. Another unfortunate trend in the church today is that many victims of these prophets of doom are unwilling to accept that they are victims of these men of the underworld. They have become so attached to their prophets that they see nothing wrong in what these

evil prophets do. They even stake their all to protect the integrity of such false prophets.

While it is relatively easy to rescue someone in the bondage of these evil men who are willing to be free, it is challenging to save those who do not accept they are in bondage. They resist every attempt to help them and prefer to live in their cocoon of an alternate reality. The good news is that no matter the effort of Satan and his cohorts against the church, it shall end in vain. The Bible says in *Matthew 16:18-19 (KJV)*, *And I say also unto thee, That thou art Peter, and upon this rock I will build my church; the gates of hell shall not prevail against it. And I will give unto thee the keys of the kingdom of heaven: and whatsoever thou shalt bind on earth shall be bound in heaven: and whatsoever thou shalt loose on earth shall be loosed in heaven.*

Whatever the gates of hell opened against the church shall not prevail. Gates of occultic manipulation and deception are some of the gates opened against the church of God today, and while some destined for perdition will fall away, the church will remain and fulfill the mandate of God on her. Finally, it is good to examine oneself daily, using the Word of God as the standard. Check yourself and ensure you do not unconsciously involve yourself in occultic practice.

2 Corinthians 13:5 (KJV) says: Examine yourselves, whether ye be in the faith; prove your own selves. Know ye, not your own selves, how that Jesus Christ is in you, except ye be reprobates?

One way of self-examination, especially in a family, is by examining God's word together as a family, keeping the light on the family altar burning. Confession should be made if any anomaly is noticed, and such anomaly should be dealt with in the place of prayer. As a church, self-examination will only come when the Word of God is held in high esteem. Sincere undiluted word of God should be preached, and the fire emanating from such sermon will shut every threatening gate of hell up. I pray that every gate of hell opened against you and your church be shut forever in Jesus' name.

Chapter Four

An Exposition of Matthew Chapter Five.

According to Saint Matthew, the fifth chapter of the gospel is a popular portion of the Bible. It is known as "The Beatitude" or "The Teaching" on the point of Olive. It is believed to have been written out by Apostle Matthew as an account of teaching by the Lord Jesus Christ. It is put together as the fifth chapter of the book of the gospel of Matthew and broken into forty-eight beautiful verses.

The teaching touched a lot of subjects and therefore should be classified into smaller groups for the convenience of study. There are a lot of significant facts about The Beatitude. For instance, interestingly, the account suggests that Jesus Christ taught this wonderful lesson spontaneously. Nothing in the report indicated that he was prepared for such a detailed and unique exposition. We shall look at this beautiful chapter from the gospel according to Saint Matthew segment by segment. *Matthew 5:1-2 (KJV) And seeing the multitudes, he went up into a mountain: and when he was set, his disciples came unto him: And he opened his mouth, and taught them, saying,*

Here it appears the crowd influenced Jesus Christ's decision to go to the small mountain. And even though He had a crowd around Him, His target audience remained His disciples. He was focused on His twelve disciples, knowing they would continue from where he would stop. Once He found a comfortable place to sit, Jesus Christ began to teach the men around him with a preference for His disciples.

The following nine verses are the main body of The Beatitude and the most discussed in the chapter. They start with the word "Blessed" and pronounce the reward on certain key characters a true Christian should display. We shall look at them further.

Matthew 5:3 (KJV) Blessed are the poor in spirit: for theirs is the kingdom of heaven: It states the reward of those who are lowly in spirit (Matthew 11:28) as the kingdom of heaven. Therefore, being poor in the spirit is a criterion for making heaven. To be poor in spirit neither refers to a financial state nor a state of being less spiritual, but it is similar to meekness. The English expression may not be very distinct, but it is understandable.

Matthew 5:4 (KJV) Blessed are they that mourn: for they shall be comforted: It is not the wish of Jesus Christ that we suffer loss. Therefore, we have an assurance in Him that He can comfort us in our moments of grief. One could further buttress this with His promise to send us the Holy Spirit, whom He describes as "The comforter."*(John 15:16)*.

Matthew 5:5 (KJV) Blessed are the meek: for they shall inherit the earth: Meekness is a state of humility or being moderate, not boastful, able to take things as they come. Jesus Christ says here that the meek shall inherit the earth. It means when you are moderate, gentle, and not boastful; you have no business being poor in life, provided you have the Lord Jesus Christ.

Matthew 5:6 (KJV) Blessed are they which do hunger and thirst after righteousness: for they shall be filled: The desire of Jesus Christ is that we hunger and thirst for righteousness, and here the promise is that we shall be filled. It is worthy of note that righteousness here is a general term that includes holiness and consecration.

Matthew 5:7 (KJV) Blessed are the merciful: for they shall obtain mercy: This verse is one of the most direct. It is a case of "you get what you give." If you are merciful, then you will obtain mercy. However, it is worth noting that the word "mercy" in the Bible is never far from forgiveness for sins. It can also be related to acts of kindness. But the pleasant thing about this verse is that you get what you give.

Matthew 5:8 (KJV) Blessed are the pure in heart: for they shall see God: This refers to those who have a heart of purity; whose minds are purged of the filth of this world. *Isaiah 64:6* readily comes to mind here. If our righteousness is like a filthy rag and it is out of the heart that issues of life emanate *(Prov 4:23),* then having a heart of purity before God should merit seeing God. Maybe not physically, but eventually, our sojourn on earth will end.

Matthew 5:9 (KJV) Blessed are the peacemakers; for they shall be called the children of God. One would logically expect the reward of those who make peace to live a peaceful life, but that will not be Biblical. *John 16:33 (KJV) says, "These things I have spoken unto you, that in me ye might have peace.* In the world ye shall have tribulation: but be of good cheer; I have overcome the world." The express word of Jesus Christ here is that we SHALL have tribulations in the world. Therefore, it is apt to say the peacemakers shall be called sons of God. If Jesus Christ is the prince of peace, then peace-loving Christians should be called children of God.

Matthew 5:10-11 (KJV) Blessed are they which are persecuted for righteousness sake: for theirs is the kingdom of heaven.

Blessed are ye, when men shall revile you, and persecute you, and shall say all manner of evil against you falsely, for my sake.

These two verses talk about the reward for suffering in the name of Christ. The Bible admonishes that we should not suffer as a murderer or a thief but for the name of Jesus Christ.

1 Peter 4:15-16 (KJV): But let none of you suffer as a murderer, or as a thief, or as an evildoer, or as a busybody in other men's matters.

Yet if any man suffers as a Christian, let him not be ashamed; but let him glorify God on this behalf.

The call of Jesus is for every Christian to focus on the crown while carrying the cross and to put our minds on the beauty of the flower while enduring the thorns. No sacrifice accepted for the sake of Christ is in vain. At the appropriate time, the reward shall come *(Galatians 6:9)*. In *Matthew 5:12*, Jesus Christ says that the reward of those persecuted for His name's sake shall be great in heaven.

The following four verses are the salt and light segments of the expository. Here Jesus Christ makes a metaphorical comparison between a true child of God and salt, then light. This section sheds light on the expectation of the Lord for us as Christians concerning what effect we should have on people around us and the world at large.

Matthew 5:13 (KJV) Ye are the salt of the earth: but if the salt has lost his savor wherewith shall it be salted? It is thenceforth good for nothing, but to be cast out, and to be trodden under foot of men.

Salt is a seasoner; once it loses its seasoning effect, it is useless. Likewise, as Christians, Jesus desires that we flavor the world around us. That we add quality to life on earth and not be sucked into the activities of men then forget what we are originally called to be on earth. The last line of this verse hints that once a Christian loses his value and expected effect, the very people he is dedicated to influencing positively are the same people who will trample him underfoot.

Matthew 5:14 (KJV) Ye are the light of the world. A city that is set on an hill cannot be hid.

The day a man declares for Christ by becoming born again, he is marked in hell. The struggle to win him back to the camp of people heading for destruction begins. Therefore, a Christian is expected to be a light unto the world but be aware he can't be hidden from Satan and his demons.

Light can mean salvation, enlightenment, freedom, knowledge, and deliverance, among many other possibilities. Christians are expected to be all of these and more to the souls of unbelievers around them.

Jesus Christ says in *John 9:5 (KJV)*: *As long as I am in the world, I am the light of the world.*

John 1:5 (KJV) adds: *And the light shineth in darkness; and the darkness comprehended it not.*

We are expected to follow our father's footsteps by being a light to the darkness of this world, filled with the assurance that the more we shine, the more we overcome the darkness of ignorance, confusion, and wickedness of bondage of the devil.

Matthew 5:15 (KJV) Neither do men light a candle, and put it under a bushel, but on a candlestick; and it giveth light unto all that are in the house.

When a man is called to an assignment, God gives him a platform to do that to which he is called. When a candlestick is used, it is given a pedestal to do what it can do best.

The work of Christians like this candlestick is to repel the darkness of this world. *Isaiah 60:1 (KJV)* states thus: *Arise, shine; for thy light is come, and the glory of the LORD is risen upon thee.*

No matter how good a candlestick may be, no matter the quality of the wax, it needs a source of fire to set it into action. Likewise, a Christian needs the rising of the glory of the Lord upon him before he can brighten his world. To grow in the race of Christianity and the work to which we are called, we need that infusion of power and grace *(Malachi 4:2)*. No wonder Jesus instructed His disciples to tarry in Jerusalem until they are endued with power from on high. Afterward, they could win souls, having been transformed through the Pentecostal experience with the Holy Spirit.

Matthew 5:16 (KJV) Let your light so shine before men, that they may see your good works, and glorify your Father which is in heaven.

Jesus Christ commands that we let our light shine so that men may be drawn by our good works and glorify God. One significant thing about this verse is that it is one of the few places where the Bible encourages an outward show of one's ability or gift. Christians are to do their best to shine the glorious light of Christ to repel darkness and thereby liberate ignorant men who yet walk in the darkness of this world.

From verse 17 to verse 48, Jesus shed light on some common sayings and laws. He started by assuring His listeners that He had no intention of destroying the law as they knew it then but to fulfill it. Fulfilling the law in this context does not mean that Jesus was to carry out all the laws mentioned, but He established a better understanding of the laws and expectations in the minds of all who heard Him and even more.

Matthew 5:17-19 (KJV) Think not that I am come to destroy the law or the prophets: I am not come to destroy, but to fulfill.

For verily I say unto you, till heaven and earth pass, one jot or one tittle shall in no wise pass from the law, till all be fulfilled.

Whosoever, therefore, shall break one of these least commandments, and shall teach men so, he shall be called the least in the kingdom of heaven: but whosoever shall do and teach them, the same shall be called great in the kingdom of heaven.

Verse 19 is a further confirmation that Jesus has no intention of changing the ancient landmarks laid down by the forefathers of what we now know as the Christian faith *(Prov 22:28)*. He kicks against adulteration of the law and every form of heretic teaching, contradicting the will of God for His children.

There is also a little mystery hidden in the last line of verse 19, which is often ignored. The last line says whosoever keeps these commandments and teaches others to do the same; such a person shall be great in the kingdom of heaven. Observing the laws and teaching others to do the same is a sure avenue to greatness in heaven.

Matthew 5:20 (KJV) For I say unto you, That except your righteousness shall exceed the righteousness of the scribes and Pharisees, ye shall in no case enter into the kingdom of heaven.

At the time of this teaching, the Pharisees were the custodian of the law. Therefore, when the law of Moses comes up for discussion, so do the Pharisees. At that time, there was a running battle between Jesus Christ and the Pharisees over their vague and biased interpretation of the laws of Moses. Jesus accused them several times of being hypocrites and biased. Hence, He made them the yardstick for gauging whether one is a candidate for the kingdom of heaven or not. After that, Jesus then picked the laws one after the other to polish the understanding of men concerning these laws.

Matthew 5:21-22 (KJV) Ye have heard that it was said by them of old time, Thou shalt not kill; and whosoever shall kill shall be in danger of the judgment:

But I say unto you, That whosoever is angry with his brother without a cause shall be in danger of the judgment: and whosoever shall say to his brother, Raca, shall be in danger of the council: but whosoever shall say, Thou fool, shall be in danger of hellfire.

Here, Jesus Christ made it clear that the danger of judgment is not only in killing another person. Anger towards another without a just cause could attract grave consequences. Also, calling another man created by God nothing or worthless or saying such a man is without value can attract punitive measures. Finally, He also says here that calling another a fool can make one lose his salvation. This is partly because these offenses can indicate the minds of the person engaging in them. The word of a man reflects his heart.

Matthew 5:23-24 (KJV) Therefore if thou bring thy gift to the altar, and there rememberest that thy brother hath ought against thee; Leave there thy gift before the altar, and go thy way; first, be reconciled to thy brother, and then come and offer thy gift.

This portion's significance is the Pharisees' greed at the time. They were concerned with people bringing gifts, not minding if such people were in right standing with God or not. Jesus Christ thus declares that you must make peace with people you have misunderstandings with before your sacrifice or gift can be accepted by God. Another side to this portion is that since it is the tradition for men to bring gifts to the temple occasionally, if they must make peace with their enemies before such gifts could be accepted, they will be forced to make peace more often. It was a fantastic conflict resolution strategy that the Pharisees did not accept.

Matthew 5:25-26 (KJV) Agree with thine adversary quickly, whiles thou art in the way with him; lest at any time the adversary deliver thee to the judge, and the judge deliver thee to the officer, and thou be cast into prison.

Verily I say unto thee, Thou shalt by no means come out thence, till thou hast paid the uttermost farthing.

The law at the time had no place for compassion. Once a man is deemed guilty, he is made to face the consequences. Therefore, Jesus Christ admonishes that faithful men who may be indebted to others should resolve their debt issues before being forced before the law.

Matthew 5:27-28 (KJV): Ye have heard that it was said by them of old time, Thou shalt not commit adultery:

But I say unto you, That whosoever looketh on a woman to lust after her hath committed adultery with her already in his heart.

The two verses above highlight one of the sharpest differences between the law as it was before Jesus Christ and when Jesus Christ came in the flesh. It was then difficult to imagine lusting after a woman to fornicating with the same woman. It must have made the people of those days feel cheated as they had to bear the guilt of what they perceived they had not done.

Jesus Christ, however, was seeing beyond the physical and considering the power of the mind and what effect thoughts could have on an individual. Therefore, it is safe to say every lewd thought of men is considered a wrongdoing. For instance, sitting at the altar and picturing the nakedness of a woman in church with a negative motive surely should be a sin and not be encouraged.

Matthew 5:29-30 (KJV) And if thy right eye offend thee, pluck it out, and cast it from thee: for it is profitable for thee that one of thy members should perish, and not that thy whole body should be cast into hell.

And if thy right hand offend thee, cut it off, and cast it from thee: for it is profitable for thee that one of thy members should perish, and not that thy whole body should be cast into hell.

The following two verses, as can be seen, instruct that we do away with any aspect of our lives that may cause us to err before God. The idea is that a part should be lost rather than the whole.

A minor detail often missed out here is the emphasis on "right" as in "right eye" and "right hand."Right here refers to 'dominant' or 'the most important because most people have a dominant right side. It emphasizes that the erring part, no matter how important, should be done away with if it will take the whole body to hell.

Matthew 5:31-32 (KJV): It hath been said, Whosoever shall put away his wife, let him give her writing of divorcement:

But I say unto you, That whosoever shall put away his wife, saving for the cause of fornication, causeth her to commit adultery: and whosoever shall marry her that is divorced committeth adultery.

In this portion of The Beatitude, Jesus Christ moves to plug the leeway left open by the law of Moses for easy divorce. He understands how marriages are easy targets for the devil and how he was exploiting the ease of writing a piece of document for that purpose. Jesus Christ, therefore, put a condition on the issue of divorce, in this case, fornication. His statement suggests that men must have issued divorce notices on frivolous claims and resolvable matters in the past. We also need to consider that some men will use flimsy excuses to put away a wife they consider 'no longer beautiful. 'Therefore, the decision of Jesus Christ to make this statement is a massively welcomed one that has saved several marriages in the past two thousand years.

Matthew 5:33-37 (KJV) Again, ye have heard that it hath been said by them of old time, Thou shalt not forswear thyself, but shalt perform unto the Lord thine oaths:

But I say unto you, Swear not at all; neither by heaven; for it is God's throne:

Nor by the earth; for it is his footstool: neither by Jerusalem; for it is the city of the great King.

Neither shalt thou swear by thy head, because thou canst not make one hair white or black.

But let your communication be, Yea, yea; Nay, nay: for whatsoever is more than these cometh of evil.

To forswear means to renege or go back on one's promise or words. A common bone of contention then was the issue of people swearing on oath and then going back on it, especially when there is no evidence or proof of the oath.

While the Scribes and Pharisees busy themselves with determining if the individuals under examination took the said oath or not, Jesus Christ had a contrary opinion. Jesus Christ admonishes that; believers should not swear or take oaths. The last verse also suggests that we should be so sincere in our lifestyle and words that men could afford to take us by our words when we say "Yea" or "Nay."

The last few verses are what I call the over-correction verses. In medical practice, over-correction refers to placing a corrected, previously deformed body part in an overcorrected position. When such part heals up, it reverts a little, leaving it in a perfect position. This is common in the correction of lower limb deformities.

Verses 38 to 47 analyze how a Christian can display the principle of over-correction, which, even if it reverts a little, still leaves the believer in a correct position.

Matthew 5:38-47 (KJV) Ye have heard that it hath been said, An eye for an eye, and a tooth for a tooth:

But I say unto you, That ye resist not evil: but whosoever shall smite thee on thy right cheek, turn to him the other also.

And if any man will sue thee at the law, and take away thy coat, let him have thy cloak also.

And whosoever shall compel thee to go a mile, go with him twain.

Give to him that asketh thee, and from him that would borrow of thee turn not thou away.

Ye have heard that it hath been said, Thou shalt love thy neighbor, and hate thine enemy.

But I say unto you, Love your enemies, bless them that curse you, do good to them that hate you, and pray for them which despitefully use you, and persecute you;

That ye may be the children of your Father which is in heaven: for he maketh his sun to rise on the evil and on the good, and sendeth rain on the just and on the unjust.

For if ye love them which love you, what reward have ye? do not even the publicans the same?

And if ye salute your brethren only, what do ye more than others? Do not even the publicans so?

The last verse is short but pregnant with meanings. It calls for perfection from Christ's audience and suggests that perfection is possible. More importantly, all that had been discussed in what is now known as "The Beatitude" is a recipe for perfection.

The Beatitude will continue to play a significant role in

Christianity and the expectation of Christ on Christians.

How do these all relate to false prophets and false teachers? The teachings of Matthew 5 are some of the areas of Christianity most bastardized by false prophets and teachers.

For instance, some false prophets encourage revenge; the beatitude refutes that. Some false prophets promote divorce, but Jesus Christ restricts that as well. False prophets and teachers often attack other positive virtues of this wonderful portion of the Bible, but discerning believers will see through their deceptions.

While it may be unwise to stay back to patch up an abusive marriage, it must be noted that the devil is still in the business of attacking unions through false prophets. A believer should prayerfully seek the face of God before making major life decisions; issues concerning marriage can not be exceptions to this rule. Testimonies abound of people who opted for divorce and never remained the same. The will of God is for couples to weather the storms of marriage together and live to share their stories of victories in their old age.

Chapter Five

An Exposition on Galatian Chapter Six.

The sixth chapter of the letter of Paul to the Galatians is the last chapter of the letter. It can be broadly divided into two parts: The first part has to do with one's personal responsibility as a believer and an encouragement to help other Christians who have fallen into sin; the latter part has to do with Paul's final words to the Galatians.

Galatians 6:1 (KJV) Brethren, if a man be overtaken in a fault, ye which are spiritual, restore such an one in the spirit of meekness; considering thyself, lest thou also be tempted.

Paul's introduction here suggests he was aware of some of the Galatians being "overtaken in a fault." The nature of the fault may not have been spelled out, but it is a minor fault rather than a grave sin.

The word "overtaken" also suggests an offense that overran the individual rather than a willful or habitual sin. It is a case where the individual slips into sin rather than being lured by lust. Paul also admonishes those who are spiritual, or I can paraphrase by saying those who are healthy spiritually should help bear up the fallen brethren. Another interesting fact is that Paul did not regard the fallen brethren as people who have fallen away from the faith but as people who still belong to the fold of the believers in Galatia but need help to find their feet again. He also encouraged the fallen brethren to be restored in meekness, not with aggression or threats of punitive measures. They should be gently ushered back in line like innocent strayed chicks. The first verse ended with caution for the spiritual brothers themselves to be careful lest they be tempted as their brothers. It is not news that some people in history have fallen into the same error they seek to correct, hence Paul's concern for the spiritual brethren of the church of Galatia.

Galatians 6:2 (KJV) Bear ye one another's burdens, and so fulfill the law of Christ.

Paul also took his advice on helping the fallen brethren by encouraging them to bear one another's burden. By so doing, they will fulfill the law of Christ. What sort of burden was Paul referring to? Paul's mention of the men overtaken by a fault suggests these men may have burdens they bear, causing them to be overtaken by a fault. Such burden maybe struggles with sin or weights, which can easily lead to sin, as mentioned in *Hebrews 12:1 (KJV): "Wherefore seeing we also are compassed about with so great a cloud of witnesses, let us lay aside every weight, and the sin which doth so easily beset us, and let us run with patience the race that is set before us" Such weights or burdens slow down a believer's Christian race and can quickly become a distraction taking our eyes off the cross on which Christ hangs.* No wonder *Hebrew 12:2* then follows with *"Looking unto Jesus the author and finisher of our faith...".*

A weight can be a behavioral addiction, like exaggeration while talking; it can be a love for food or a health problem. All these can make one sin eventually, even though they may not be sin.

The law of Christ in *Galatians 6:2* refers to John 13:34-35 (KJV): A new commandment I give unto you, That ye love one another; as I have loved you, that ye also love one another.

By this shall all men know that ye are my disciples if ye have love one to another.

One deep point to note is the challenge Jesus Christ poses to every believer. He clearly states that love among the brethren is the way to know they are Christ's followers. The natural question that comes to mind is if present-day Christians can boast of such love. If they cannot, will it be right for believers to claim still to be followers of Jesus Christ?

Galatians 6:3 (KJV) For if a man thinks himself to be something when he is nothing, he deceiveth himself.

Here Paul talks about pride. When a man arrogates himself beyond where God has placed him, he risks a disastrous fall. Perhaps, some of the spiritual brethren in Galatia were looking down on the less spiritual, necessitating Paul to make such a statement.

There is no worse deception than thinking yourself to be what you are not. Even a lunatic sometimes thinks himself to be normal and doing well in every sphere of life. Therefore, a proud man and a lunatic have something in common.

Proverbs 16:18 (KJV) says Pride goeth before destruction, and an haughty spirit before a fall.

This takes the danger of pride, especially among brethren in a Christian fold.

Galatians 6:4-5 (KJV) But let every man prove his own work, and then shall he have rejoicing in himself alone, and not in another. For every man shall bear his burden

Here, after shunning pride and an aura of thinking they are what they are not, Paul admonished further that each man should prove his achievement or contribution to the work of God. He also said they should rejoice in their achievement and that each should bear his burden before God.

There are many situations in the Bible where churches are judged by their works, for instance, the seven churches in the book of Revelations. But here, Paul is reminding us that the race to the kingdom of God is an individual race. It is a race that requires that you present your deeds before God for approval.

2 Corinthians 5:9-10 (KJV): Wherefore we labor, that, whether present or absent, we may be accepted of him. For we must all appear before the judgment seat of Christ; that everyone may receive the things done in his body, according to that he hath done, whether it be good or bad.

Galatians 6:6-10 talks of doing good to other men within the household of faith. Here, Paul boldly stated that while it is good to be good to others, it is better to do good to fellow believers. It is perhaps the only place in the Bible where such is so clearly stated.

Galatians 6:6 (KJV): Let him that is taught in the word communicate unto him that teacheth in all good things.

Paul taught that the ones taught should be supportive of their teachers. He said it should be done regarding all good things. Paul refers to a fundamental Christian principle that those who feed people spiritually should, in turn, be rewarded with support from the people they feed. It is also Biblical that he who lives by the word eat by the word.

1 Corinthians 9:11-13 (KJV): If we have sown unto you spiritual things, is it a great thing if we shall reap your carnal things?

If others are partakers of this power over you, are not we rather? Nevertheless, we have not used this power; but suffer all things, lest we should hinder the gospel of Christ.

Do ye not know that they which minister about holy things live of the things of the temple? and they who wait at the altar are partakers with the altar?

Therefore, it is appropriate if believers reciprocate love to their spiritual leaders and teachers through physical support, either monetary or otherwise.

Galatians 6:7-8 (KJV) Be not deceived; God is not mocked: for whatsoever a man soweth, that shall he also reap. For he that soweth to his flesh shall of the flesh reap corruption, but he that soweth to the Spirit shall of the Spirit reap life everlasting.

This is the most popular portion of the book of Galatians. It is popularly used in churches as a reference to encourage brethren to sow to the work of God.

In Chapter 7, Paul said no man should live in the deception of thinking God does not know his effort and lack of it in the church of God. Then he followed with the assurance that a commensurate reward would follow every action of the believer. It does not necessarily mean that if a man buys a chair for the church, he will also get a chair in return, but a commensurate reward will be meted out to the person, which may be in another form. Someone who pays his neighbor's medical bill may find himself miraculously saved from a car crash. It is the reward for his past good works. It is, however, only the Holy Spirit who knows what reward is commensurate with what good work.

Verse 8 is a continuation of verse 7; it clarifies what reward to expect depending on what seed is sown. Every seed planted by a farmer is expected to bring out fruit like itself. No farmer sows rice and expects maize. What will germinate must be of the same species as what was planted.

Likewise, spiritually, whatever is sown determines what will be reaped. He who sows bountifully shall also reap bountifully. But he who sows sparingly will no doubt reap sparingly.

Proverbs 11:25 (KJV): The liberal soul shall be made fat: and he that watereth shall be watered also himself.

This verse says that when you sow, you shall reap. Galatians 6:8, however, is a bit deeper. It is a clear explanation that it is not just about sowing, the nature of the seed you also sow matters. You shall reap a perishable reward if you sow or invest in the flesh. However, if you sow to the Spirit, you shall of the Spirit reap a spiritual reward. By extension, the decision on the nature of the seed to be sown lies with the sower, but God determines the reward.

Galatians 6:9 (KJV): And let us not be weary in well doing: for in due season we shall reap, if we faint not.

A believer is expected to do good and should never be tired of so doing. As inevitable as the seasons of sowing and reaping are, so is the certainty of a time to reap after sowing into the things of the Spirit of God.

"In due season" indicates that a reward will be due at some point. However, when the reward is due may not be what can be calculated. It is the Holy Spirit who determines when the time for reward is due.

Galatians 6:10 (KJV): As we have therefore opportunity, let us do good unto all men, especially unto them who are of the household of faith.

This verse is the crux of this segment of Galatians 5. It is a clear indication of what sort of ground to sow on. It reminds me of the parable of the sower, where seeds were sown on different lands with varying conditions. The results were equally various. Here, we were told to sow on a fertile ground represented by the life of men of the household of faith.

"As much as lieth in you" means with all your might or ability. Or, with all your capability or all that lies within your control, do good to people. "Especially unto them, who are of the household of faith" is an expression that nudges the doer's heart of good in a particular direction.

While it is good to do good unto all men, it is better to direct the good doing towards people of the household of faith. Silently, there is an undertone of more blessing coming from seed sown back into the household of faith as opposed to seed sown generally. In other words, based on this verse, it is better you bless a fellow believer than spend your resources on unbelievers. Not that a believer should not be a blessing to an unbeliever, but one option is clearly better than the other according to the advice of Apostle Paul and the leading of the Holy Spirit n him.

However, it is logical to reason along the line proffered by this statement. It is wiser to assist a fellow believer who can also help in influencing other believers and so continue the positive chain of influence, rather than an unbeliever who might spend the resources invested on him to destroy even the believer who is his benefactor.

Galatians 6:11-13 (KJV): Ye see how large a letter I have written unto you with mine own hand. As many as desire to make a fair shew in the flesh, they constrain you to be circumcised; only lest they should suffer persecution for the cross of Christ. For neither they themselves who are circumcised keep the law; but desire to have you circumcised, that they may glory in your flesh.

In Galatians 6:11, Paul indicated that he had written the letter to the Galatians with his hand. The custom then was to dictate to someone else who helps with the writing, and then he will write a little aspect of it or just a sort of postscript. We can see this in *1 Corinthians 16:21,* where he indicated that the salutation area of the letter was done by his hand. Also, in *Colossians 4:18,* we see a similar indication.

Contrary to the above examples, Paul said he had written the "large" letter with his hand. Some school of thought takes it that large here refers to the size of the alphabets, which may be because he had a sight problem, but it could also refer to the actual volume of the letter, that is, the relative volume he had to write with his hand to the Galatians.

There were some members of the believers in Galatia who belonged to a higher class and wished to have believers from gentile backgrounds circumcised in their flesh. Unfortunately, the purpose of these influential groups of men was not to glorify God but to make a public show of the uncircumcised believers of gentile background.

Not only that, another negative motive of this class of men among the believers was to avoid persecution if they publicly supported that circumcision of the heart is enough and that of the flesh may not be necessary. The stand of this group of believers put the unfortunate few believers with a gentile background in a dilemma. They were caught between the law of circumcision and the law of grace.

Apostle Paul, however, appears to be more concerned with the self-glorification of the legalistic group of believers. The following verse hinted at what Paul supported, which was in line with the law of grace rather than circumcision.

Galatians 6:14-16 (KJV) But God forbid that I should glory, save in the cross of our Lord Jesus Christ, by whom the world is crucified unto me, and I unto the world. For in Christ Jesus neither circumcision availeth anything, nor uncircumcision, but a new creature. And as many as walk according to this rule, peace be on them, and mercy, and upon the Israel of God.

Apostle Paul took a stand here, electing that he would not take glory in the trauma of others but in the cross of Jesus Christ and what it stands for.

In verse 14, the stand of Apostle Paul was further proven by his statement on physical circumcision. It does not matter if an individual, especially when already an adult, is physically circumcised or not. What matters is the circumcision and rebirth of the heart.

In verse 16, Paul blessed many who chose to follow the path of faith in the circumcision of the heart rather than physical circumcision.

In verse 17, Paul declared that no man should trouble him henceforth as he bore in his body marks that point to the fact he was conformed to His suffering.

2 Corinthians 11:23-25 (KJV): Are they ministers of Christ? (I speak as a fool) I am more; in labors more abundant, in stripes above measure, in prisons more frequent, in deaths oft. Of the Jews five times received I forty stripes save one.

Thrice was I beaten with rods, once was I stoned, thrice I suffered shipwreck, a night and a day I have been in the deep;

Galatians 6:18 (KJV): Brethren, the grace of our Lord Jesus Christ be with your spirit. Amen.

It was only fitting to close such a loaded letter with a goodwill greeting. The latter part of the chapter highlights the presence of certain brethren with ulterior motives different from Christ's. They seek glory but not of Christ, and Apostle Paul was quick to dissociate himself from their school of thought.

Much as the false prophet in present-day Christendom, they preach with vigor, are active in church, and seek the highest positions of honor, but they are not of God.

As analyzed in the early part of the chapter, everybody shall have a reward for his work someday, good or bad; these false teachers of the law of God shall not be exempted.

Chapter Six

The Holy Spirit.

And when the day of Pentecost was fully come, they were all with one accord in one place. And suddenly there came a sound from heaven as of a rushing mighty wind, and it filled all the house where they were sitting. And there appeared unto them cloven tongues like as of fire, and it sat upon each of them. And they were all filled with the Holy Ghost and began to speak with other tongues, as the Spirit gave them utterance. Acts 2:1-4 (KJV).

The Holy Spirit is one of the three personalities of the Trinity. In other words, the personality referred to as the Holy Spirit by Christians is an equal partner in the Holy Trinity. The Holy Trinity comprises God the Father, God the Son, and God the Holy Spirit. God the Father is the creator of life as we know it today and all within it.

In the beginning God created the heavens and the earth. Genesis 1:1 (KJV).

The whole of Genesis, chapter one, narrates God the Father's creative power *(Genesis 1: 1-31)*. It tells of how He created the universe in six days. It is worthy of note that the Bible started with this account.

The first reference to the Trinity was made in verse 26 of the same Genesis chapter 1.

And God said, Let us make man in our image, after our likeness: and let them have dominion over the fish of the sea, and over the fowl of the air, and over the cattle, and over all the earth, and over every creeping thing that creepeth upon the earth. Genesis 1: 26 (KJV).

Who was God referring to in this portion of the creation account? It is not likely created beings that He made lesser than the man to be created. He had to be referring to beings far more superior to the being he had created.

For thou hast made him a little lower than the angels, and hast crowned him with glory and honor. Psalms 8:5 (KJV).

Thou madest him a little lower than the angels; thou crownedst him with glory and honor, and didst set him over the works of thy hands: Hebrews 2:7 (KJV).

It is safe to conclude that God the Father called on God the Son -who will later make the sacrifice of atonement for the beings to be created and God the Holy Spirit -who will later become the permanent channel of communication between God the Father and man. God the Son is an equal member of the Trinity. He is the one who volunteered to come to the world in human form and died for Adam's helpless race. Adam is the first man created by God, and all other humans came through him. The fall of Adam, his chase out of the garden of Eden, and the need for Christ to come and die to bridge the gap is an account we shall skip here, as the concentration is on the Holy Spirit.

The next day John seeth Jesus coming unto him, and saith, Behold the Lamb of God, which taketh away the sin of the world: John 1:29 (KJV).

But God commendeth his love toward us, in that, while we were yet sinners, Christ died for us. Romans 5:8 (KJV).

The Holy Spirit is the least understood of the three personalities of the Trinity. This is because the Bible gave a lot of accounts of God the Father in the Old Testament, and then in the New Testament era, Jesus Christ came to the world in the form of a man, hence the familiarity of man with Jesus Christ.

In His part, the Holy Spirit has never appeared to any man in the form of a human, and neither is there a large account about Him in the Bible. To make the understanding of the person and function of the Holy Spirit more complex, an experience of the Holy Spirit usually requires a certain level of spirituality on the part of man. Therefore, because man is carnal and not spiritual, experiencing the Holy Spirit or things pertaining to the Holy Spirit becomes extremely difficult.

But the natural man receiveth, not the things of the Spirit of God: for they are foolishness unto him: neither can he know them, because they are spiritually discerned :1 Corinthians 2:14 (KJV).

There are many misconceptions about the Holy Spirit, one of which is the reference to Him as the third member of the Trinity because He is inferior to the other two. There is no biblical reference to this effect. While it could be logical to imagine God the Father as higher than the other two members of the Trinity, just because He is the Father or because the other two appear at times to be extensions of Him, the fact remains there is no proof for that.

We can take solace in the understanding that, as humans, our knowledge of such high spiritual matters is limited. When we get to heaven someday, we shall better understand the relationship between the three personalities, for we shall be like Christ, see Him as He is, and understand the Trinity better.

Beloved, now are we the sons of God, and it doth not yet appear what we shall be: but we know that, when he shall appear, we shall be like him; for we shall see him as he is.1

John 3:2 (KJV).

While many may want to argue about the person of the Holy Spirit, such arguments are usually baseless. What God has revealed to us about Himself should suffice, and whatever He decides we do not need to know at this age belongs to Him.

The secret things belong unto the LORD our God: but those things which are revealed belong unto us and to our children forever, that we may do all the words of this law. Deuteronomy 29:29 (KJV).

What are the popular misconceptions about the Holy Spirit?

There are many misconceptions about the Holy Spirit, just as earlier stated. It is, therefore, essential for every true child of God to rise in understanding of the things of the Spirit of God to the level of seeing the Holy Spirit as the Spirit of God in us. He is the same Spirit that brought Jesus back to life and was sent to continue with man after the ascension of Jesus back to heaven.

There is a fact about the Holy Spirit in the Bible that Christians hardly consider. It is the Holy Spirit who guarantees our inheritance in God.

In whom ye also trusted, after that, ye heard the word of truth, the gospel of your salvation: in whom also after that ye believed, ye were sealed with that Holy Spirit of promise,

Which is the earnest of our inheritance until the redemption of the purchased possession, unto the praise of his glory.

Ephesians 1:13-14 (KJV).

Some misconceptions about the Holy Spirit are as follows:

1. That the Holy Spirit has no personality but is a force: This can be disproved by the account of Genesis 1: 26-27.

Genesis 1:26-27 (KJV): And God said, let us make man in our image, after our likeness: and let them have dominion over the fish of the sea, and over the fowl of the air, and over the cattle, and over all the earth, and over every creeping thing that creepeth upon the earth.

So God created man in his own image, in the image of God created he him; male and female created he them.

In verse 26, God used the expression "Our image," meaning the other members of the Holy Trinity are persons with personalities like God the Father Himself. And in verse 27, the expression changed to "on His own image" and "in the image of God" after man had been created. This means, indeed, the personality and features of man not just physically have a blueprint from the three persons of the Holy Trinity.

2. That the Holy Spirit only comes and goes just like a feeling: In the era of the Old Testament, the Holy Spirit then used to visit specific men of God and then leave once the purpose of His visit was accomplished. We see that in the cases of some prophets and Samson and Daniel.

But now bring me a minstrel. And it came to pass, when the minstrel played, that the hand of the LORD came upon him:

2 Kings 3:15.

This is an account of Elisha; Holy Spirit was called down on Him with the aid of music and musical instrument. However, in the New Testament, the mode of the relationship between the Holy Spirit and man has dramatically improved. The Holy Spirit now resides inside us.

Ezekiel 36:27 (KJV): And I will put my Spirit within you, and cause you to walk in my statutes, and ye shall keep my judgments, and do them.

1 Corinthians 6:19 (KJV): What? Know ye not that your body is the temple of the Holy Ghost which is in you, which ye have of God, and ye are not your own?

Romans 8:9 (KJV): But ye are not in the flesh, but in the Spirit, if so be that the Spirit of God dwells in you. Now, if any man has not the Spirit of Christ, he is none of his.

3. The Holy Spirit is only present when you feel something like goosebumps: The Holy Spirit is a permanent resident in any genuine Christian. True, certain unusual feelings may herald the move of the Holy Spirit, but the Holy Spirit cannot be limited to that. He operates in diverse ways. *Genesis 28:16 (KJV): And Jacob awaked out of his sleep, and he said, Surely the LORD is in this place, and I knew it not.*

In the account above, Jacob did not experience goosebumps or even sense the presence of God the Father or the Holy Spirit. Yet God revealed Himself to him.

4. The Holy Spirit is only present during a spectacular phenomenon: The Holy Spirit guides us into all truth, whether huge or small, spectacular, or otherwise. *John 16:13 (KJV): Howbeit when he, the Spirit of truth, is come, he will guide you into all truth: for he shall not speak of himself; but whatsoever he shall hear, that shall he speak: and he will shew you things to come.*

Furthermore, He may not necessarily appear in extraordinary phenomena but in a still small voice. *1 Kings 19:12-13 (KJV): And after the earthquake a fire; but the LORD was not in the fire: and after the fire a still small voice.*

And it was so, when Elijah heard it, it was so that he wrapped his face in his mantle, went out, and stood in the entering of the cave. And, behold, there came a voice unto him, and said, What doest thou here, Elijah?

5. That He is authoritative and aggressive: Contrary to such beliefs, the Holy Spirit is not only gentle and quiet, but He is also gentle. No one can give what he does not have. *Galatians 5:22 (KJV): But the fruit of the Spirit is love, joy, peace, longsuffering, gentleness, goodness, faith,*

6. That because the Holy Spirit is gentle, He cannot be forceful. This is another aberration in the understanding of men concerning the Holy Spirit. The Holy Spirit, although gentle, is a person and can make decisions. He has His behavior and is not always as soft as people think. *Mark 1:11-12 (KJV): And there came a voice from heaven, saying, Thou art my beloved Son, in whom I am well pleased*

And immediately the Spirit driveth him into the wilderness.

After Jesus Christ was baptized, there was a need for Him to go through a series of temptations by the devil in the wilderness. It is not a decision that is easy for flesh and blood to take, hence the need for the Holy Spirit to 'drive' him on into the wilderness.

Different authors of the Bible at other times refer to the Holy Spirit in diverse ways, using slightly different expressions, depending on the Bible Version. Some of them with references include:

a. The Holy Spirit.
Acts 1:8 (NIV): But ye shall receive power, after that the Holy Spirit is come upon you: and ye shall be witnesses unto me both in Jerusalem, and in all Judaea, and in Samaria, and unto the uttermost part of the earth.

Also, in *1Corinthians 6:19 (NIV), Acts 2:38 (NIV),* and *Romans 5:5 (NIV).*

b. The Spirit.
Galatians 5:22 (KJV): But the fruit of the Spirit is love, joy, peace, longsuffering, gentleness, goodness, faith,

Also, in *Mark 1:12* and *Romans 8:16.*

c. The Spirit of God or The Spirit of The Lord.
2 Corinthians 3:17 (KJV): Now the Lord is that Spirit: and where the Spirit of the Lord is, there is liberty.

Also, Romans 8:14 (KJV) and *1 Corinthians 2:14.*

d. His Spirit
Ephesians 3:16 (KJV): That he would grant you, according to the riches of his glory, to be strengthened with might by his Spirit in the inner man;

Also, 1 John 4:13 (KJV)

e. Holy Ghost.
Acts 1:8 (KJV): But ye shall receive power, after that the Holy Ghost is come upon you: and ye shall be witnesses unto me both in Jerusalem, and in all Judaea, and in Samaria, and unto the uttermost part of the earth.

Also, *Acts 10:38 (KJV), Mark 13:11 (KJV), Romans 15:13 (KJV)*, and *2 Pet 1:21 (KJV)*

f. God's Spirit
1 Corinthians 3:16 (KJV): Know ye not that ye are the temple of God, and that the Spirit of God dwelleth in you?

g. My Spirit
Genesis 6:3 (KJV): And the LORD said, My Spirit shall not always strive with man, for that he also is flesh: yet his days shall be an hundred and twenty years.

Why was the Holy Spirit sent?
The Holy Spirit was sent to continue where Jesus Christ stopped in the flesh. In other words, the Holy Spirit was sent by God the Father through God the Son, Jesus Christ, to help us stay connected to God after the ascension of Jesus Christ.

But the Comforter, which is the Holy Ghost, whom the Father will send in my name, he shall teach you all things, and bring all things to your remembrance, whatsoever I have said unto you. John 14:26 (KJV).

There are several reasons why God the Father had to send the Holy Spirit to the world. These reasons are all tied to giving us a sense of belonging in Christ Jesus and helping to keep us linked to God the Father despite our imperfections and limitations.

Unlike the days of old when the Holy Spirit seemed to only work with a few selected men of God, otherwise called prophets, the grace to have the Holy Spirit is now open to all.

Titus 2:11-12 (KJV) says: For the grace of God that bringeth salvation hath appeared to all men,

Teaching us that, denying ungodliness and worldly lusts, we should live soberly, righteously, and godly in this present world;

The grace is now available; the decision has been firmly put in the hands of individuals.

The Bible says in *John 1:12 (KJV): But as many as received him, to them gave he power to become the sons of God, even to them that believe on his name:*

The Holy Spirit activates the power mentioned above. Hence, He cannot be detached from a believer's authority in Christ Jesus. To a considerable extent, the power of a believer in

Jesus Christ is expressed through the working of the Holy Spirit.

There are several instances of the actions of the Holy Spirit in the Bible.

1. He descended like a dove on Jesus Christ at baptism, driving him into the wilderness to be tempted by the devil.

And straightway coming up out of the water, he saw the heavens opened, and the Spirit like a dove descending upon him: And there came a voice from heaven, saying, Thou art my beloved Son, in whom I am well pleased. And immediately the Spirit driveth him into the wilderness. Mark 1: 10-12 (KJV).

2. He visited the disciples at Pentecost as a mighty rushing wind and was seen as cloven tongues of fire on the heads of all present.

Acts 2:1-3 (KJV): And when the day of Pentecost was fully come, they were all with one accord in one place. And suddenly there came a sound from heaven as of a rushing mighty wind, and it filled all the house where they were sitting. And there appeared unto them cloven tongues like as of fire, and it sat upon each of them.

3. He caused Phillip to vanish and reappear elsewhere.

Acts 8:38-40 (KJV): And he commanded the chariot to stand still: and they went down both into the water, both Philip and the eunuch; and he baptized him. And when they were come up out of the water, the Spirit of the Lord caught away

Philip, that the eunuch saw him no more: and he went on his way rejoicing. But Philip was found at Azotus: and passing through he preached in all the cities, till he came to Caesarea.

There are several other accounts of the actions of the Holy Spirit in the Bible. Many Christians walking with God have also experienced the Holy Spirit in action. Many reports abound on how the Holy Spirit has mysteriously healed or delivered Christians from death. People have miraculously known things they were not taught or have revelations that science or the five senses cannot handle. The presence of the Holy Spirit in a child of God and His ability to act cannot be overemphasized.

The functions of the Holy Spirit are numerous and can hardly be classified.

1. He plays a role in divine birth.
And the angel answered and said unto her, The Holy Ghost shall come upon thee, and the power of the Highest shall overshadow thee: therefore also that holy thing which shall be born of thee shall be called the Son of God: Luke 1:35 (KJV).

2. He guides us into all truth and gives us revelation of the future.
Howbeit when he, the Spirit of truth, is come, he will guide you into all truth: for he shall not speak of himself; but whatsoever he shall hear, that shall he speak: and he will shew you things to come: John 16:13 (KJV)

3. He comforts and counsels us.
John 14:16 (KJV): And I will pray the Father, and he shall

give you another Comforter, that he may abide with you forever

4. He helps our infirmities and helps us to pray.
Romans 8:26 (KJV): Likewise the Spirit also helpeth our infirmities: for we know not what we should pray for as we ought: but the Spirit itself maketh intercession for us with groanings which cannot be uttered.

But ye, beloved, building up yourselves on your most holy faith, praying in the Holy Ghost, Jude 1:20 (KJV).

5. He teaches us and brings the teachings to our remembrance.
But the Comforter, which is the Holy Ghost, whom the Father will send in my name, he shall teach you all things, and bring all things to your remembrance, whatsoever I have said unto you.

John 14:26 (KJV)

6. He gives us spiritual gifts
Now concerning spiritual gifts, brethren, I would not have you ignorant. 1 Corinthians 12:1 (KJV).

7. He empowers us to bear the fruits of the Spirit.
But the fruit of the Spirit is love, joy, peace, longsuffering, gentleness, goodness, faith, meekness, temperance: against such there is no law. Galatians 5:22-23 (KJV).

There are lots of other functions of the Holy Spirit in the body of Christ. Some of them include: He testifies of Jesus *(John*

15:26), He baptizes *(Matthew 3:11)*, He gives revelations in the form of visions and dreams *(Acts 2:17)*, He quickens our mortal body *(Romans 8:13)*, He grants us access to God the Father *(Ephesians 2:18)*, and so on.

The Holy Spirit also bestows gifts to faithful Christians. In *1 Corinthians 12:1-11*, several gifts of the Spirit were listed, like Word of Wisdom, word of knowledge, Faith, Gifts of healing, working of miracles, Prophecy, Discerning of spirits, Diverse tongues, and Interpretation of tongues.

However, there are several other gifts that the Holy Spirit can give to Christians in the body of Christ. They are all for the edification of the body of Christ. Every true child of God needs to know that true divine inspiration only comes from God. There are counterfeit spirits mimicking the Holy Spirit, but the Holy Spirit is one.

Many false prophets get inspiration from demonic beings, but history has proven that they do not end well. No matter how attractive the wonders and counterfeit miracles of the false prophets may be, a true child of God should never emulate such.

It is only the Spirit of God that gives life, and everything carnal does not profit eventually *(John 6:63a)*. Every gift also that is not of God through the Holy Spirit will lead to destruction, and that is always the end of every false prophet claiming to be a true prophet of God.

Chapter Seven

Religious Malpractice and National Development:

Nigeria as a case study. How Religious Malpractice Has Affected the Peace of Nigeria.

Nigeria has three major religions: Christianity, Islam, and the Traditional Religion. The latter was the original religion of the people before the coming of Islam and Christianity. The traditional religion comprises different forms of worship; there are many gods under the traditional religion, such as the god of Iron, Thunder, Sea, Sun, etc. This religion encourages ritual and blood sacrifices at times, and sometimes animals or humans can be offered as a sacrifice to appease their gods. That is the major downside of traditional religion; many religions are under that umbrella. Islam is one religion that is poorly practiced in Nigeria; even though the Holy Prophet Mohammed (SAW) said clearly that religion is not by force, his followers practicing the religion in the northern part of the country seems to have a very low tolerance level for people of other faith, and even discriminate between them and other Muslim from the southern part of the country. They consider them as not religious enough. One significant malpractice of Islam is the miscarriage of ideology and the jihadi tendency of some among them. They believe that fighting and defending their God is a holy thing. However, God does not need a man to fight or defend him in the real sense. The Jihad ideology has made the entire world a difficult place to live; it has threatened the universe's peace. The United States, for example, has spent hundreds of billions fighting this wrong ideology which has given birth to terrorist groups across the world.

This is an undeniable example of how people have misrepresented the ideals and values of Islam.

In Christianity, on the other hand, the leading malpractice of the religion is the destruction of souls through financial exploitation and intellectual, emotional, and even mental slavery. These are propagated through the Pentecostal sect. The founders are not answerable to anyone, not even the church members. Even when a board of trustees is in place, in most cases, it is just a figurehead board with no influence on the church's leadership.

Not to say that all Pentecostal churches are not functioning well in Nigeria, as some are still well structured. Nigeria's leading Christian regulatory bodies are the Christian Association of Nigeria (CAN) and the Pentecostal Fellowship of Nigeria (PFN). These two bodies have not effectively ensured the proper practice of Christianity in Nigeria. They are ineffective and have not served in the interest of Christians but in the interest of Church owners; sounds more like Religious Oligarch.

We hear of Pastors under the umbrella of PFN involved in different forms of scandals, and these Pastors are not even investigated or disciplined. However, it is another case among the non-Pentecostals as they have structures that can handle such situations. Some disciplinary measures include asking the Pastor to step aside for investigation. Further disciplinary actions are then taken if the Pastor is found guilty.

Growing up in the Evangelical Church Winning All (ECWA), I saw the church taking disciplinary actions against Pastors and church members who got involved in acts not expected of a Christian. Such persons were suspended from church activities and handed over to the church council of elders for counseling which could last six months or more. During counseling and probation, they assess their conduct and determine if there is true repentance before they are restored back to ministry. I can proudly say that this is still being practiced in the church.

Compared to some Pentecostal churches, Pastors accused of misconduct, even with proof, will not step aside. They are not answerable to anybody, not even the Pentecostal Fellowship of Nigeria (PFN). Some members even defend such misconduct of their pastors, and they move on like the misconduct never happened. The system is so corrupt now that even its members who are supposed to expose such wrongdoings for disciplinary action will instead keep them secret. Such members indirectly encourage misconduct in the church. They encourage misconduct such as fraud, sexual harassment, etc. Some eventually come out crying foul when they become the victims of these questionable pastors. They continue to encourage such evil acts as long as they are not the victims.

A typical example of this is a Nigerian actress, who accused her Pastor of lodging her sister in a hotel for about three days and being sexually involved with her. Unfortunately for her, she had earlier engaged her Pastor in a conversation where she entrusted her sister into his hands. As usual, he devoured her as he did to other people. The saddest part was that he did the same to her sister; wolves will always be wolves. They will never behave, as they have become ardent at their dastardly acts. These are people who will always misbehave and are not ready to repent.

Strangely enough, some of the souls they have kept in bondage are also not ready to be liberated. This is because some of them have been hypnotized with demonic powers. When people try to deliver them from bondage, they attack those who intend to set them free. That is how bad the situation has become.

More souls are falling into the hands of gods of men than in the hands of men of God the creator. These false men of God are supposed to lead people to Christ, but instead, they lead people to themselves.

Sometimes I wonder why people are comfortable worshiping where they do not feel the presence of God. In *Psalm 46:10*, the Bible says, *"Be still and know that I am God: I will be exalted among the nations, I will be exalted in the earth.*

People no longer seek God in this era; instead, they seek any form of solution to their problems. Unfortunately, they do not know that some solutions will only compound their conditions. The counterfeit solutions they get are indirectly from the devil, and only the things that come from God are the ones that give peace of mind.

Jeremiah 33:3, the Bible says: *Call unto me and I will answer you and tell you great and unsearchable things you do not know (NIV)*. This Bible verse speaks volumes; it tells us to trust God and depend on Him for wisdom. Many Christians still trust men because such men are erroneously referred to as men of God. People, especially those still young in the faith, tend to trust and know them more than God. They believe that such men are closer to God than they are and that God will hear the prayers of such men than theirs. It is wrong to have such a mindset. We should know God by ourselves and not believe anyone has access to God more than we do; God expects us to have fellowship with him without any third party.

Apart from churches under the Pentecostal Fellowship of Nigeria, there have been cases of scandals and misconduct in other churches within other blocs under the Christian Association of Nigeria. There have been cases of financial misappropriation, rape, and even people dying during deliverance sessions. While it is common knowledge that no church is a perfect place, the body of Christ cannot afford to be ignorant of the devil's wiles. Punitive measures may not solve every problem, but churches and their governing boards should not be afraid to wield the big stick.

It should also be noted that these occurrences in the church are just a reflection of the greater society. Therefore, such discussion will not be complete without making mention of other malpractices in the religious community at large.

The Oxford dictionary defines religion as belief in a spiritual or metaphysical reality, often including at least one deity, accompanied by practices and rituals about the belief.

As earlier noted, there are diverse types of religion worldwide. Different people, races, tribes, and ethnic groups have various religious practices with which they identify. In most cases, the classification of religion involves many generalizations of several more minor faiths. For instance, traditional belief in Africa as a classification is a generalization of many smaller religions involving an uncountable number of deities. A single traditional religion in Africa may boast of over two hundred gods, suggesting variation in the mode of worship and demands of these deities.

All known religion identifies with the need for peace in society. However, their practice differs in the area where they believe such peace should be achieved. While most Christian sects believe in grace and forgiveness of sin, other religions believe in instant capital judgment.

Such a difference in religious beliefs means there will always be inter-religious conflict in a multi-religious society like Nigeria.

The destructive effects of religious malpractice on national development can be looked at from different perspectives, using the Federal Republic of Nigeria as a case study. Some of these malpractices are general, while some are specific to certain religions. For clarity, even though much has been considered about such inconsistencies in a Christian sect, a holistic perspective is still needed for better understanding.

Some of the malpractices involving most if not all the various religious bodies, in general, are as follows:

1. Inter-religious rivalry: Rivalry among the various religions in the country does not appear to be going away anytime soon. It is not out of place to hear of

people practicing different religions in the same area of society bickering over space, disturbance, and noise pollution. While the level of tolerance of other faiths is improving in the developed cities, the rural areas still experience a lot of skirmishes emanating from inter-religion intolerance.

2. Religious bodies are trying to influence government at different levels: It is unfortunate that certain religious bodies shamelessly try to manipulate the political arena of their country. While it is not wrong for a Christian to be involved in politics, the church should be careful about being partisan or openly supporting a candidate. Chance is, there will be supporters of rival parties or candidates in the church, too; as a result, excessive political involvement can only breed bad blood.

3. They preach about wealth and prosperity rather than righteousness and good morals: Several false pastors now preach what they perceive people want to hear. With the current hardship in society, people want to listen to messages that will assure them of their coming wealth. As a result, these false men of God lie to them and exploit them by making them part with enormous amounts of money as seeds for the expected financial boom.

4. They are flirting with the government rather than cautioning them: All the prominent men of God in Nigeria have paraded the country's seat of power to curry favor or accept gifts from money to expensive

cars. Unlike the prophets of old who called kings to order, most of our present-day prophets only worry about their bellies. As a result, while kings called prophets like Elisha Father, present-day governments treat most clerics from different religions as puppets to be used to brainwash their teeming followers.

5. Religious leaders now compete with one another in the number of jets and expensive schools they own: Many prominent clerics now travel in expensive private jets regardless of the state of the church's welfare. Many members of churches cannot afford the costly schools belonging to the church, which the members' contributions have built.

Some religious malpractices peculiar to the Christian sects in Nigeria are:

1. There is no mechanism to check the excesses of erring pastors who own these churches.

2. Increase in the number of mushroom churches with questionable doctrines and bizarre claims.

3. There is no uniformity in message delivery resulting in some preaching inflammatory messages that are not of God.

4. Inter-church rivalry. For instance, Pentecostals detest indigenous churches like the Celestial Church of Christ.

5. Practices of some indigenous churches bothering on fetish activities that are not biblical

Some religious malpractices are, however, particular to the Islamic sect too.

1. Fanatic tendencies and extremism.
2. Lack of informative teaching about the religion to the worshippers.
3. Retaining traditional customs in religion.
4. Inciting the youths with the sermon of violence.
5. Religious culture that opposes western education.

The traditional religious group cannot be left out of this discussion, as they too are a part of the society and are not blameless in this matter under consideration,

Some malpractices involving worshippers of indigenous gods in Nigeria are but are not limited to these points.

1. There is no central body to check the activities of worshippers of different gods identified in Nigeria.
2. An alarming increase in cases of money rituals involving human sacrifices.
3. An increase in numbers of false priests with no power expected of them as priests of African gods.

4. Increase in cases of scamming activities involving people claiming to be priests of traditional gods.

5. External infiltration from countries like India.

6. Erosion of the line between herbal practice and black magic.

7. The use of cunningness to make people join an occultic association.

All the above-listed malpractices have an undesired effect on the Nigerian society causing massive underdevelopment and growth retardation in some areas.

Some of the harmful effects of these malpractices are as follows.

1. Increase in fanatic segregation among youths in the society.

2. Reduction in inter-religion tolerance and pockets fights between religious sects.

3. Increased rate of killings and terrorist groups creation.

4. Retardation of economic growth following destructions of properties and farms due to societal unrest.

5. Creation of an atmosphere of insecurity.

6. Political struggles with religious undertones.

7. Discouragement of youths from religious seriousness.

8. Increase in numbers of false pastors, false imams, and false traditional priests.

The damaging effect of poor religious practice on the development of Nigeria cannot be swept under the carpet. The news is always awashed with negative reports about religious malpractice and its undesired effects. The most worrying fact is not that these things are happening but that nothing has been done to put these religious bodies in check. My sincere prayer is that God himself will win over the heart of His representatives in the country and help them begin the right thing in Jesus' name.

Chapter Eight

Alliance Between the False Prophets and Authorities in Power.

Psalms 2:1-5, 8-9, 11 (KJV): Why do the heathen rage, and the people imagine a vain thing?
The kings of the earth set themselves, and the rulers take counsel together, against the LORD, and against his anointed, saying, Let us break their bands asunder, and cast away their cords from us.
He that sitteth in the heavens shall laugh: the Lord shall have them in derision. Then shall he speak unto them in his wrath, and vex them in his sore displeasure.
Ask of me, and I shall give thee the heathen for thine inheritance, and the uttermost parts of the earth for thy possession.
Thou shalt break them with a rod of iron; thou shalt dash them in pieces like a potter's vessel.
Serve the LORD with fear, and rejoice with trembling.

We no longer know who a false prophet or false preacher is. They range from self-acclaimed men of God, genuinely called men of God who turned bad halfway, to pure agents of darkness who are in the church to bring it to disrepute. The latter group continues to get involved in scandals after scandals; they continue their strange religious practices and yet continue to gain popularity until Satan deems their time is up.

From the stand of the Bible on the person and activities of antichrists, we can easily conclude that these false prophets parading as children of God are antichrists. The Oxford dictionary says an antichrist works against the teachings of Christ. Even though many of these prophets outwardly preach from the Bible, they work against the teachings of Christ and the principles of Christianity in their closets.

Little children, it is the last time: and as ye have heard that antichrist shall come, even now are there many antichrists; whereby we know that it is the last time.
1 John 2: 18 (KJV)

For instance, they preach the need for repentance and even sanctification. They, however, accept money from crooks without even bothering to ask after the source of the money, let alone preach repentance. They preach from *1 John 2: 15-17*, asking their members not to love the world nor the wealth of the world, but they do not only amass wealth, but they also frolic with the ungodly high and mighty of the society.

They preach the power of healing in the name of Jesus, asking men to put church stickers on their doors for protection. Meanwhile, they rely heavily on medications, not able to pray off a minor headache. They are spoken of in *2 Timothy 3: 5 as having a form of godliness but denying the power thereof.* The verse instructs us that from such people, we should turn away.

Jesus Christ knows about these false religious heads who profess to be closer to God than anyone else. They are quick to point out faults in others, but they are far worse in their closets. They are quick to correct others, but they are not only evil; they even dine and wine with the devil.

Woe unto you, scribes and Pharisees, hypocrites! for ye pay tithe of mint and anise and cumin, and have omitted the weightier matters of the law, judgment, mercy, and faith: these ought ye to have done, and not to leave the other undone.

Ye blind guides, which strain at a gnat, and swallow a camel.

Woe unto you, scribes and Pharisees, hypocrites! for ye make clean the outside of the cup and the platter, but within they are full of extortion and excess.

Thou blind Pharisee, cleanse first that which is within the cup and platter, that the outside of them may be clean also. Matthew 23:23-26 (KJV).

Even though every Christian knows of the coming emergence of the Antichrist, the Bible makes us know that there are smaller antichrists, and they are already amongst us in disguise. They do their opposition work against the teachings of Christ in subtle ways unnoticed by many.

Before the emergence of the Antichrist, many other events must take place. Among these events are the imposition of the mark of the beast on people's forehead and wrists, universal currency, and religion.

There is news about a conspiracy to make the world comply with a single religion. Even though there may not be solid proof of such a move, it is an expected sign of the end time. Not too long ago, at the birthday party of a renowned man of God, where the pope himself was present, the celebrant openly proposed the unification of the whole religions of the world. Could this be the proof of the conspiracy? Your guess is as good as mine. When top men of God come together to form a megachurch that swallows all other churches, then they begin to impose rules that will contradict the teachings of Christ. This quest is consistent with the definition of antichrists.

Before the mega-alliance, smaller alliances will begin, indicating what is to come at the end of the days. False men of God are beginning to wink at politicians and people in power. It was unthinkable years ago that an honest man of God would travel a long distance to visit and spend days with a tyrant.

The expectation from such men of God with Bible references is for them to tell the tyrant the truth. But what we see today are men of God visiting top politicians, sitting together, eating together, appearing in pictures, laughing, and having a wonderful time. You cannot help but wonder how much money the politician must have given the so-called men of God. As was noted earlier, they are whited sepulchers and broken cisterns with no grace to offer. These false men of God are antichrists in disguise, and their identity shall be made known in due time.

Another exciting sign that these devil puppets are not real men of God is that their ministries are barren lands. They own the most prominent churches, and their appearances preach opulence and elegance rather than righteousness and uprightness, but their ministries are barren grounds. Money invested into such ministries to further the Gospel of Jesus Christ in the form of tithe, offering, and kingdom partnership yields nothing.

While the Bible promises great blessing on those faithful in paying tithe and offering, sowing in these ministries is like sowing on hot, dry rocks.

Bring ye all the tithes into the storehouse, that there may be meat in mine house, and prove me now herewith, saith the LORD of hosts, if I will not open you the windows of heaven, and pour you out a blessing, that there shall not be room enough to receive it. Malachi 3:10 (KJV).

In the Gospel according to *James, chapter 4* in *verse 3*, the Bible says: *Ye ask, and receive not, because ye ask amiss, that ye may consume it upon your lusts.*

I can infer that it will not be wrong to put it slightly differently by saying: You plant and reap not because you have down on barren rocks.

Men sow in these ministries but remain impoverished while the pastors continue to amass wealth from the sweat of their followers. This lack of results is because such seeds went down on the wrong grounds. A cursed land cannot breed blessings; a ground dedicated to the things of the devil cannot be a breeding ground of grace for a child of God.

An evil politician and a false prophet share a lot in common. They both engage in what the Bible calls the doctrine of Nicolaitans. And Jesus Christ himself said He hates it.

Nicolaitan is a term from two Greek words, "Nicao" and "Lao," and it means "Kill laity."

Revelation 2:15-16 (KJV): So hast thou also them that hold the doctrine of the Nicolaitans, which thing I hate. Repent; or else I will come unto thee quickly, and will fight against them with the sword of my mouth.

The bad politicians who promote policies that cause the sincere populace to suffer and the clergy who cheat them out of their hard-earned resources are fruits from the same tree. They are all involved in the doctrine of "Kill laity" or "kill the innocent followers of Christ."

Many politicians today are greedy baskets that are never satisfied. They keep taking but are never contented. Some divert what is meant for a whole community or nation to their private account, yet they keep looking for more. No wonder the Bible says: *Better is a little with righteousness than great revenues without right (Proverbs 16: 8).*

The present-day alliance between the false prophets and the political authorities is one of friendship with benefits. Both parties have one thing or the other to gain from the partnership. It is a shame that men who claim to be of God could stoop so low as to be involved in such an ungodly alliance.

The politicians gain from this unholy alliance in the following ways:

1. The politicians get an opportunity to win men to their camp who could help them fool their followers into supporting the politicians.

2. The false prophets canvass the politicians in their places of worship, confusing them into pledging their support for their leader's political allies.

3. The politicians also enjoy prophecies from the false prophets who use diabolical means to foretell the future or manipulate the election results to favor them.

4. There are cases where youths gather to mob some politicians who are performing poorly. Still, these politicians approach the youths and convince them otherwise with black magic or enchantment from some false clerics.

5. Most bizarre of all these alliances is that some politicians make the clerics fight the opponents through spiritual means. Many politicians have died mysteriously for not having solid spiritual backing against their enemies.

The false prophets or clerics also stand to gain from this evil alliance. They stay connected with the politicians knowing they could use their position to gain some perishable things in this world.

The false prophets gain the following from the alliance between them and the political class:

1. Cheap popularity as a friend to someone in authority.

2. The false prophet gets to influence policymaking decisions.

3. The false prophets get their candidates in choice positions when job opportunities arrive.

4. The false prophets get paid by the politicians for their spiritual backing on getting into power or killing their rivals.

5. The false prophets also get political positions for their faithful followers through the politicians.

It is an evil symbiotic relationship where both parties gain a great deal. Both the false prophets and the politicians shake hands and are left satisfied. Their gain, however, is the loss of their sincere counterparts in the body of Christ.

Pastors or prophets who do not have alliances with politicians are not famous or influential. Also, if such pastors do not squeeze out money from their members and thus appear less flamboyant, they are quickly classified as poor men of God. The tendency for people to keep comparing pastors will always be there. Unfortunately, it is not easy to compare two people in terms of who is more anointed, but it is possible to tell who drives the better car and whose family appears more comfortable.

It shows that the more these false men of God gain ground in the church, the more toxic the environment becomes for the sincere men of God. To make matters worse, as the false prophets increase, they come together in an alliance against the few good men of God. They throw propaganda at the few sincere prophets and do all they can to make life difficult for them. It is easier for these false prophets to do these as they are often more affluent, more popular, and can sweet tongue the world into seeing things their way.

Their agenda in some churches is to frustrate the few sincere men of God so they can dominate the place. Sincere men of God who have been through such experience will recount how emotionally draining it can be. It creates the feeling of not being appreciated, and Satan will always suggest resigning to such true men of God.

The result is a gradual takeover of some once vibrant Christian sects by false prophets with no vision. The serene atmosphere of the Spirit of God has been replaced with wild, often worldly singing without the Holy Spirit. They no longer sing Spirit-led songs, hymns, and worship that carry the eternal message and are from the direct breath of the Holy Spirit. Instead, sick churches rely entirely on songs composed from the five senses of men that appeal to emotion rather than the inner spirit of man.

As children of God, we should never be ignorant of the devil's devices through these evil men who parade as holy men of God. When so-called men of God gang up against a single man of God, one must look at such situations closely. Often, it is the single man of God being ganged up against that is a true man of God. This is a recurring decimal that should not continue to go unchecked. The succor of the true man of God, who in this case is a sheep among wolves, is that, in the long run, God will fight for him.

Many are the afflictions of the righteous: but the LORD delivereth him out of them all. He keepeth all his bones: not one of them is broken. Psalms 34: 19-20 (KJV).

Also, in *Psalms 2* from *verse 1*, the Bible offers protection to the few oppressed sincere men of God among the increasingly evil men in suits parading as men of God on the altar these days. Even though their coming together increased their collective strength, victory over them is still certain for the true men of God.

Behold, they shall surely gather together, but not by me: whosoever shall gather together against thee shall fall for thy sake.

Behold, I have created the smith that bloweth the coals in the fire, and that bringeth forth an instrument for his work; and I have created the waster to destroy.

No weapon that is formed against thee shall prosper; every tongue that shall rise against thee in judgment thou shalt condemn. This is the heritage of the servants of the LORD, and their righteousness is of me, saith the LORD. Isaiah 54: 15-17 (KJV).

The end time is truly here. All the signs are springing up; some are easy to see, while some need a little scratching of the surface to be exposed. Alliances are going on; supposed men of God and tyrant politicians now walk and work hand in hand. I tell you, such a relationship cannot be of God except the tyrant politician had repented.

Almost all the prominent pastors in Africa, with Nigeria as a case study, have visited and prayed for the tyrant rulers of their countries. You want to picture the exact words they share in their meetings and the words they utter in such prayers. Do they remember to tell God to strike such politicians dead if they fail to repent? Probably not. Do they warn the politicians to desist from their wicked ways because of the danger of hell fire? Probably not, else they would not be smiling and hugging after such meetings. Do they make it clear to these political rulers that God is not happy with the oppression of His children? Obviously not, else their relationships would not remain cordial if the tyrant political rulers are not repentant.

The end time truly is here, and every evil alliance against the body of Christ shall be destroyed in Jesus' name.

A man of God who was the head of the PFN of his country in Africa was always seen in the company of prominent politicians. He started as a fire-breathing young man of God, much loved by all children of God regardless of denomination. Now, he appears in public in all black wear, complete with dark glasses and several funny-looking rings on his fingers.

This man of God has private jets and several luxury cars and has not been heard to preach in public in a long time. Recently, some Christian sects complained about fraternizing with politicians, but he brushed aside their observations and concerns. Not too long ago, this supposed man of God was implicated in a deal involving his private jet being used to convey guns from another country to his own country. No matter his intention or role in this matter, it is not the will of God that his children be involved in such alliances with the world.

Many of these false prophets start well but eventually show their true colors.

They went out from us, but they were not of us; for if they had been of us, they would no doubt have continued with us: but they went out, that they might be made manifest that they were not all of us. 1 John 2: 19 (KJV).

I pray that this shall not be the testimony of the few men of God who are still standing firmly in the faith in Jesus' name. There is a need for us Christians to pray for our pastors and leaders. We should give special attention to prayer for the few sincere men of God going through massive oppression in the church.

The grace of God will keep us away from the power of the devil fighting against the church in Jesus' name (Amen).

Chapter Nine

Has God Really Spoken?

God hath spoken once; twice have I heard this; that power belongeth unto God. Psalms 62:11 (KJV).

The sovereign God of heaven speaks, and He is still in the business of speaking to His people. Even though He is the Almighty God, the maker of heaven and earth, the creator of the universe, the all-knowing and all-perfect God, He still manages to come down to the level of an ordinary mortal like man to communicate with us. The Psalmist testified that all power belongs to Him and that God said it once, but he heard it twice. It shows how wondrous and, at the same time, flexible our God can be.

The Bible records that He spoke, and His voice sounds like thunder.

Job 37:5 (KJV): God thundereth marvelously with his voice; great things doeth he, which we cannot comprehend.

The first account of God speaking in the Bible birthed light.

And God said, Let there be light: and there was light. Genesis 1: 3 (KJV).

How does God speak?

Over the years, God has spoken to His children in various ways. Initially, He spoke face to face with His main representative; over time, several other options of hearing from God have been graciously made available by Him.

Some of the ways through which the Almighty God has spoken to men in the past are as follows:

1. Audible voice.
Isaiah 30:21 (KJV): And thine ears shall hear a word behind thee, saying, This is the way, walk ye in it, when ye turn to the right hand, and when ye turn to the left.

2. Heart instruction.
Psalms 16:7 (KJV): I will bless the LORD, who hath given me counsel: my reins also instruct me in the night seasons.

3. Dream.
2 Chronicles 7:12 (KJV): And the LORD appeared to Solomon by night, and said unto him, I have heard thy prayer, and have chosen this place to myself for an house of sacrifice.

4. Angelic visitation.
Judges 6:11-12 (KJV): And there came an angel of the LORD, and sat under an oak which was in Ophrah, that pertained unto Joash the Abiezrite: and his son Gideon threshed wheat by the winepress, to hide it from the Midianites.

And the angel of the LORD appeared unto him, and said unto him, The LORD is with thee, thou mighty man of valor.

5. Through a prophet.
Judges 6:8-9 (KJV): That the LORD sent a prophet unto the children of Israel, which said unto them, Thus saith the LORD God of Israel, I brought you up from Egypt, and brought you forth out of the house of bondage;

And I delivered you out of the hand of the Egyptians, and out of the hand of all that oppressed you, and drove them out from before you, and gave you their land;

6. Inspiration from the Word of God.

7. Intuition

The fact that He is the Almighty God when He speaks does not go without a sign. Here are a few of what can happen in response to God speaking:

When He speaks

* Healing becomes the children's bread (*Psalms 107:20*).

* Circumstances change for the better (*Exodus 14:13-15*).

* Your sins are forgiven (*Luke 7:48*).

* New things begin to manifest, (*Isaiah 43:19*).

* Dead bones rise again (*Ezekiel 37:1-7*).

* Deliverance is sure (*Jonah 2:10*).

* Storms are stilled (*Matthew 8:26*).

* Harvest abounds (*Luke 5:5*).

The above are just a few remarkable things that have followed God's spoken word. Whatever way He has chosen to speak, great signs have always followed.

Before we consider the false prophets, who speak as mouthpieces of God and no signs follow, we need to compare instances of God speaking in the Bible and what obtains today.

1. *Genesis 1:3 (KJV): And God said, Let there be light: and there was light.*

God commanded light on a world shrouded in darkness. After He spoke, the Light of day and night appeared.

2. *1 Kings 19:12-13 (KJV): And after the earthquake a fire; but the LORD was not in the fire: and after the fire a still small voice.*

And it was so, when Elijah heard it, that he wrapped his face in his mantle, and went out, and stood in the entering in of the cave. And, behold, there came a voice unto him, and said, What doest thou here, Elijah?

God spoke to Prophet Elijah in a still, small voice. The instructions God gave him that day were instrumental to him finding a successor.

3. *2 Samuel 12:7-9 (KJV): And Nathan said to David, Thou art the man. Thus saith the LORD God of Israel, I anointed thee king over Israel, and I delivered thee out of the hand of Saul;*

And I gave thee thy master's house, and thy master's wives into thy bosom, and gave thee the house of Israel and of Judah; and if that had been too little, I would moreover have given unto thee such and such things.

Wherefore hast thou despised the commandment of the LORD, to do evil in his sight? Thou hast killed Uriah the Hittite with the sword, and hast taken his wife to be thy wife, and hast slain him with the sword of the children of Ammon.

The Lord spoke through Prophet Nathan to rebuke David after he had an affair with Bathsheba and killed her husband, Uriah.

4. *Exodus 3:4-5 (KJV): And when the LORD saw that he turned aside to see, God called unto him out of the midst of the bush, and said, Moses, Moses. And he said, Here am I.*

And he said, Draw not nigh hither: put off thy shoes from off thy feet, for the place whereon thou standest is holy ground.

This is the account of Moses' experience with the burning bush. God spoke to Him through the burning bush and sent him back to Egypt to liberate the children of Israel.

5. *Acts 9:1, 4-5 (KJV): And Saul, yet breathing out threatening and slaughter against the disciples of the Lord, went unto the high priest,*

And he fell to the earth and heard a voice saying unto him, Saul, Saul, why persecutest thou me?

And he said, Who art thou, Lord? And the Lord said, I am Jesus whom thou persecutest: it is hard for thee to kick against the pricks.

God spoke to Paul on his way to persecuting the followers of Christ. It was a significant turnaround in his life as he changed his name and focus. From being the thorn of the devil in the flesh of the followers of Christ, he became perhaps the greatest evangelist Christianity has ever known.

6. *Matthew 3:16-17 (KJV): And Jesus, when he was baptized, went up straightway out of the water: and, lo, the heavens were opened unto him, and he saw the Spirit of God descending like a dove, and lighting upon him:*

And lo a voice from heaven, saying, This is my beloved Son, in whom I am well pleased.

After Jesus Christ was baptized, He heard a voice of confirmation from heaven.

This was the first instance in the Bible where we saw the trinity working together at a single location. God the Son, Jesus Christ, was baptized by water immersion; God the Father, Jehovah, spoke from heaven in approval. Then, God the Holy Spirit immediately took over, driving Jesus Christ into the wilderness to dwell there and fast for forty days and forty nights. He was also tempted there but without falling.

7. *Exodus 14:15-16 (KJV): And the LORD said unto Moses, Wherefore criest thou unto me? speak unto the children of Israel, that they go forward:*

But lift thou up thy rod, and stretch out thine hand over the sea, and divide it: and the children of Israel shall go on dry ground through the midst of the sea.

God spoke to Moses, instructing him to lead the children of Israel forward toward the Red Sea. With the Egyptian army chasing them behind, God caused the Red Sea to part into two to allow the Israelites to pass. When the Egyptian army also tried to pass through the two water bodies on both sides, the water closed in on them, destroying them and their horses.

There were instances when God spoke, and His message was perverted for selfish reasons. Some of these instances can be found in the Bible, and men still do the same to date.

Some prophets try to make money from God's gift, claiming, "He who serves at the altar eats of the proceeds of the altar. "Therefore, when God reveals a solution to a problem, they will relate same but ask for some form of monetary sacrifice from the person. Not only that, but some of them also pervert a genuine divine revelation given through another prophet for selfish gain.

The elders which are among you I exhort, who am also an elder, and a witness of the sufferings of Christ, and also a partaker of the glory that shall be revealed:

Feed the flock of God which is among you, taking the oversight thereof, not by constraint, but willingly; not for filthy lucre, but of a ready mind;

Neither as being lords over God's heritage, but being ensamples to the flock. 1 Peter 5:1-3 (KJV).

We shall examine a few of such cases from the Bible.

1. The Serpent and Eve in the garden of Eden.

Genesis 3:4-6 (KJV): And the serpent said unto the woman, Ye shall not surely die:

For God doth know that in the day ye eat thereof, then your eyes shall be opened, and ye shall be as gods, knowing good and evil.

And when the woman saw that the tree was good for food, and that it was pleasant to the eyes, and a tree to be desired to make one wise, she took of the fruit thereof, and did eat, and gave also unto her husband with her; and he did eat.

The serpent fooled her into believing she would not die after eating the forbidden fruit. However, eating the fruit resulted in spiritual death, separation from God, and the loss of His glory.

2. The old and the young prophet.
1 Kings 13:11-18 (KJV): Now there dwelt an old prophet in Bethel; and his sons came and told him all the works that the man of God had done that day in Bethel: the words which he had spoken unto the king, them they told also to their father.

And their father said unto them, What way went he? For his sons had seen what way the man of God went, which came from Judah.

And he said unto his sons, Saddle me the ass. So they saddled him the ass: and he rode thereon,

And went after the man of God, and found him sitting under an oak: and he said unto him, Art thou the man of God that camest from Judah? And he said I am.

Then he said unto him, Come home with me, and eat bread.

And he said, I may not return with thee, nor go in with thee: neither will I eat bread nor drink water with thee in this place:

For it was said to me by the word of the LORD, Thou shalt eat no bread nor drink water there, nor turn again to go by the way that thou camest.

He said unto him, I am a prophet also as thou art; and an angel spake unto me by the word of the LORD, saying, Bring him back with thee into thine house, that he may eat bread and drink water. But he lied unto him.

God genuinely sent the young prophet, and he did an excellent job of all he was sent to do until the old prophet came along. The old prophet told the young prophet that an angel had appeared to him with a message to the contrary. Either the old prophet lied outrightly, which was not clearly defined, or a demonic angel used him to destroy the young prophet with a bright future.

One significant thing for every child of God to learn from this story, among others, is the comparison between the sources of the two messages delivered to the two prophets. It was God who gave the first message to the young prophet, but an angel delivered the contrary message to the old prophet. Between God and an angel, who should a prophet believe? The result of opting to believe an angel over God is what the story ended with

3. Gehazi and Naaman.

2 Kings 5:20-24 (KJV): But Gehazi, the servant of Elisha the man of God, said, Behold, my master hath spared Naaman this Syrian, in not receiving at his hands that which he brought: but, as the LORD liveth, I will run after him, and take somewhat of him.

So Gehazi followed after Naaman. And when Naaman saw him running after him, he lighted down from the chariot to meet him, and said, Is all well?

And he said, All is well. My master hath sent me, saying, Behold, even now there be come to me from mount Ephraim two young men of the sons of the prophets: give them, I pray thee, a talent of silver, and two changes of garments.

And Naaman said, Be content, take two talents. And he urged him, and bound two talents of silver in two bags, with two changes of garments, and laid them upon two of his servants; and they bare them before him.

And when he came to the tower, he took them from their hand, and bestowed them in the house: and he let the men go, and they departed.

Gehazi, the servant of prophet Elisha, tried to play smart by double-crossing his master. He felt it was a colossal waste to allow the Syrian general to go without paying for his healing, seeing that he was a wealthy man. Gehazi ran after him and perverted the word of his master, the prophet of God. The result is that he earned himself and his lineage a curse of leprosy.

Many false prophets and false preachers of the word of God are doing far worse today. Many use cunning means to get money from unsuspecting faithful worshipers. Some twist the truth out of context to earn money from Christians, while some entirely withhold the truth as it will make their congregation realize who they are.

The most grievous problem that accompanies the work of these false prophets is the harm their punishments bring to the innocent. Often, when God visits them with his judgment, even the innocent people they prophesy to also suffer along with them.

A good example is the case of the prophet Hananiah who prophesied the freedom of the Israelites from captivity in Babylon within two years when God did not send him. Prophet Jeremiah confronted him and decreed that he would die. The Bible recorded that he died without fail in the seventh month of the same year.

Jeremiah 28:9-17 (KJV): The prophet which prophesieth of peace, when the word of the prophet shall come to pass, then shall the prophet be known, that the LORD hath truly sent him.

Then Hananiah the prophet took the yoke from off the prophet Jeremiah's neck, and brake it.

And Hananiah spake in the presence of all the people, saying, Thus saith the LORD; Even so will I break the yoke of Nebuchadnezzar king of Babylon from the neck of all nations within the space of two full years. And the prophet Jeremiah went his way.

Then the word of the LORD came unto Jeremiah the prophet after that Hananiah the prophet had broken the yoke from off the neck of the prophet Jeremiah, saying,

Go and tell Hananiah, saying, Thus saith the LORD; Thou hast broken the yokes of wood, but thou shalt make for them yokes of iron.

For thus saith the LORD of hosts, the God of Israel; I have put a yoke of iron upon the neck of all these nations, that they may serve Nebuchadnezzar king of Babylon; and they shall serve him: and I have given him the beasts of the field also.

Then said the prophet Jeremiah unto Hananiah the prophet, Hear now, Hananiah; The LORD hath not sent thee; but thou makest this people to trust in a lie.

Therefore thus saith the LORD; Behold, I will cast thee from off the face of the earth: this year thou shalt die, because thou hast taught rebellion against the LORD.

So Hananiah the prophet died the same year in the seventh month.

The children of Israel remained in captivity beyond the two years prophesied by the false prophet; they even exceeded the seventy years prophesied until Daniel realized by reason of the written record that their time in captivity was up. However, Prophet Jeremiah's prophesy about the false prophet Hananiah's death came to pass.

There are also situations when a true prophet is compelled to alter the word of God.

Jeremiah 38: 1-28 narrates an account of the prophet before the ruler of Jerusalem. He gave a prophecy about the fall of Jerusalem that made them throw him into a dungeon. When given a second chance, he still stood on what he had said earlier, even buttressing it, making it more transparent. He was thrown back into prison, which saved his life.

By the time the Babylonians came to destroy Jerusalem, they had killed almost every inhabitant of the city but spared the prisoners; after all, the prisoners were only suffering for wronging the enemies of the Babylonians. Prophet Jeremiah was spared, and he lived to his old age.

Jeremiah 38:1-2, 4, 6, 8-10, 14, 17-18, 28 (KJV): Then Shephatiahthe son of Mattan, and Gedaliah the son of Pashur, and Jucalthe son of Shelemiah, and Pashur the son of Malchiah, heard the words that Jeremiah had spoken unto all the people, saying,

Thus saith the LORD, He that remaineth in this city shall die by the sword, by the famine, and by the pestilence: but he that goeth forth to the Chaldeans shall live; for he shall have his life for a prey, and shall live.

Therefore, the princes said unto the king, We beseech thee, let this man be put to death: for thus he weakeneth the hands of the men of war that remain in this city, and the hands of all the people, in speaking such words unto them: for this man seeketh not the welfare of this people, but the hurt.

Then took they Jeremiah, and cast him into the dungeon of Malchiah the son of Hammelech, that was in the court of the prison: and they let down Jeremiah with cords. And in the dungeon there was no water, but mire: so Jeremiah sunk in the mire.

Ebed-melech went forth out of the king's house, and spake to the king, saying,

My Lord the king, these men have done evil in all that they have done to Jeremiah the prophet, whom they have cast into the dungeon; and he is like to die for hunger in the place where he is: for there is no more bread in the city.

Then the king commanded Ebed-melech the Ethiopian, saying, Take from hence thirty men with thee, and take up Jeremiah the prophet out of the dungeon, before he die.

Then Zedekiah the king sent, and took Jeremiah the prophet unto him into the third entry that is in the house of the LORD: and the king said unto Jeremiah, I will ask thee a thing; hide nothing from me.

Then said Jeremiah unto Zedekiah, Thus saith the LORD, the God of hosts, the God of Israel; If thou wilt assuredly go forth unto the king of Babylon's princes, then thy soul shall live, and this city shall not be burned with fire; and thou shalt live, and thine house:

But if thou wilt not go forth to the king of Babylon's princes, then shall this city be given into the hand of the Chaldeans, and they shall burn it with fire, and thou shalt not escape out of their hand.

So Jeremiah abode in the court of the prison until the day that Jerusalem was taken: and he was there when Jerusalem was taken.

Prophet Micaiah was another prophet who faced persecution and death over the prophecy he gave yet did not flinch.

When the king of Judah, Jehoshaphat, visited his friend Ahab, the king of Israel, their discussion soon turned to the issue of war. King Ahab asked his friend to accompany him to war to reclaim Ramoth-Gilead; King Jehoshaphat agreed but requested that they enquire from a prophet to know their fortune.

King Ahab gathered about four hundred prophets of Baal, and they all prophesied the same thing saying the king shall surely go and return victorious.

King Jehoshaphat had the discerning spirit of God in him according to *2 Chronicles 17:3*. He sensed something was not right; he knew he could not trust the prophets of Baal and requested another prophet. He wanted a prophet, not of Baal; he wanted a prophet of Jehovah, the God of Israel and Judah.

King Ahab mentioned a certain prophet Micaiah, the son of Imlah. He noted that he does not prophesy good about him and that he hated the prophet. Prophet Micaiah was called anyway.

The person sent to call the prophet warned him to be mindful of what he would say as all the other prophets had promised the king a victorious battle. Micaiah responded by swearing that he would say what the Lord told him to say.

Micaiah was not intimidated when he got to the two kings at the city gate; he maintained a straight face. Eventually, King Ahab told him about the battle in Ramoth-Gilead, wanting to know if he would return alive.

Prophet Micaiah told the king in the presence of his friend and the crowd of Baal's prophet that he would return safely, but he must have said it in derision. King Ahab saw the expression of mockery on his face and insisted the prophet should tell him the true revelation he got from God. That request opened the door for the prophet of God to pour out his heart.

He told the king that he would not return alive. After he was slapped by Zedekiah, the head of the prophets of Baal, he recounted how a spirit from heaven had come down to be a lying spirit in the mouth of all the prophets of Baal.

Even when king Ahab commanded that the prophet be thrown into prison until he returned, prophet Micaiah declared that if he returned, then he was not called of God. The rest is history. King Ahab did not return alive. He died a freak death; on some other day, he should have survived such a wound, but on that day, he did not and died as prophesied by the prophet of God. (*1 Kings 22:1-37*).

How many of our modern-day prophets can stand up to the president of their country with such harsh divine prophecy? How many prophets of today will not renege on their promise to be straightforward in the delivery of their duties as a prophet of God?

Back to our primary focus, when these false prophets speak, the question is, "Has God really spoken?"

When a prophet speaks, it is expected to happen, but today, many give end-of-the-year prophecies that do not even attempt to happen. Many say, and it never comes to pass. Many of them even avoid prophecies that can be verified by being evasive. I pray that God will give the few true prophets out there the boldness of a lion to perform their duties.

Chapter Ten

Morals Should Count for Something.

The Bible created a lot of awareness about the existence of false prophets; Jesus Christ talked about it and the apostles too. The presence of false prophets or preachers has spread worldwide, in different denominations within the body of Christ. The impact on society is incredibly heartbreaking. I have noticed the increase in the activities of false prophets and the uncountable number of lives they have destroyed and continue to destroy. I was moved to author this book to create awareness further and make people conscious of those wolves in sheep's skin.

Many online platforms have been creating this awareness; despite that, the false prophets will conspire with authorities in some countries to suppress the people's voice, especially in Nigeria and other African countries. Some of these false men of God even fight back with litigations claiming defamation of character. Fighting these men's corrupt and demonic oppression has proven extremely dangerous. They fight back with all their might and resources and even use diabolical powers to fight people trying to expose them. Their activities have sent many people out of the church, and the remaining ones have been operating under bondage; they have destroyed families and marriages in so many ways.

In Matthew 7:15-20, Jesus Christ warned that the false prophets would come in sheep's clothing, but inwardly they are wolves. Our Lord also added that people would know them by their fruits, meaning that we should be able to identify them by their activities. Despite these warnings, people still fall prey to false prophets. There are varied reasons for this.

1. Most Christians do not study the Bible: They do not understand the warnings and the instructions given. In Matthew 7:17, the Bible is clear about the kind of fruits a good tree will bear and the type of fruit a bad tree will bring. The Bible says a good tree will yield good fruit, and a bad tree will produce evil fruit. People who do not study the Bible will not understand this. Some Christians would rather listen to what they hear people preach, and unfortunately, they listen to the false prophets the Bible has warned against. These evil trees can only yield bad fruit.

2. Another reason people fall prey is that some false preachers use diabolical powers to put their members under bondage: I once listened to a man on YouTube who confessed that he and some pastors had used demonic forces to control members of a church. He said they bought three wireless microphones; one was intended to be used when they want to ask people to donate money, the other will be used when they want to preach, and whatever they ask people to do, they will obey. And they continued to destroy innocent lives.

3. Another reason people fall prey is that they trust these wolves unknowingly. Such people trust them without knowing how wicked they are. Even after they find out, some of them cannot leave because they have been hypnotized and abused and are scared of what may happen if they dare leave.

Other reasons have been mentioned earlier. The truth

remains that more reasons will continue to come up if these wicked men are allowed to operate.

In Matthew 7:19, the Bible says a tree that does not bring forth good fruit is cut down and cast into the fire; this implies that such false preachers will eventually end up in destruction and condemnation; evil can never last forever. As they always say, "Every day for the thief, one day for the owner."

Matthew 7 says, "by their fruits, you shall know them." This means our Lord Jesus Christ has given more than enough hints and concluded that we should be able to identify them. Those who cannot are responsible for their stupidity; there is no excuse for people to allow the false preachers to lead them to hell or destruction.

A true preacher of the gospel should live a transparent life; they should not be living a life filled with scandals. A "Man of God" is a man, and, understandably, he could commit some error, but they must own up to it and repent of their sins. Contrary to that, in this generation, most will try to cover their sins; they will even suppress or kill those trying to expose them. In most cases, those who eventually expose them are usually their victims or people close to the victims and people who work with them.

There are about 57 Bible verses that instruct us as Christians to live a transparent life; among them are Hebrew 4:13, 2 Timothy 2:15, and James 5:16, to mention a few.

2 Timothy 4:1-22 (NKJV) says: *I charge you therefore before God and the Lord Jesus Christ, who will judge the living and the dead at His appearing and His kingdom: Preach the word! Be ready in season and out of season. Convince, rebuke, exhort, with all longsuffering and teaching. For the time will come when they will not endure sound doctrine, but according to their own desires, because they have itching ears, they will heap up for themselves teachers; and they will turn their ears away from the truth, and be turned aside to fables. But you be watchful in all things, endure afflictions, do the work of an evangelist, fulfill your ministry. For I am already being poured out as a drink offering, and the time of my departure is at hand. I have fought the good fight, I have finished the race, I have kept the faith. Finally, there is laid up for me the crown of righteousness, which the Lord, the righteous Judge, will give to me on that Day, and not to me only but also to all who have loved His appearing. Be diligent to come to me quickly; for Demas has forsaken me, having loved this present world, and has departed for Thessalonica—Crescents for Galatia, Titus for Dalmatia. Only Luke is with me. Get Mark and bring him with you, for he is useful to me for ministry. And Tychicus I have sent to Ephesus. Bring the cloak that I left with Carpus at Troas when you come—and the books, especially the parchments. Alexander the coppersmith did me much harm. May the Lord repay him according to his works. You also must beware of*

him, for he has greatly resisted our words. At my first defense no one stood with me, but all forsook me. May it not be charged against them. But the Lord stood with me and strengthened me, so that the message might be preached fully through me, and that all the Gentiles might hear. Also, I was delivered out of the mouth of the lion. And the Lord will deliver me from every evil work and preserve me for His heavenly kingdom. To Him be glory forever and ever. Amen! Greet Prisca and Aquila, and the household of Onesiphorus. Erastus stayed in Corinth, but Trophimus I have left in Miletus sick. Do your utmost to come before winter. Eubulus greets you, as well as Pudens, Linus, Claudia, and all the brethren. The Lord Jesus Christ be with your spirit. Grace be with you. Amen.

Analyzing the above scripture, we see that Apostle Paul warned the people about false preachers. Unfortunately, some preachers started well and eventually sought power from demonic sources for financial gain. They become obsessed with the idea of expanding their ministries at any cost. They want to have mega-churches filled with worshipers at the expense of saving their souls; this has been the trend among many Pentecostal pastors in African countries like Nigeria, Ghana, and South Africa.

In the case of South Africa, most of the pastors manipulating their people seem to be from neighboring countries. The church industry appears to be booming there because the people appear to be very vulnerable to brainwashing. In the case of Nigeria and Ghana, most of the pastors involved in brainwashing the people are citizens of the country. Many have resorted to using magical powers to keep their members in bondage.

It is so bad that when people expose these fake Pastors, they come in defense aggressively. These fake pastors also influence the systemic corrupt law enforcement agencies to suppress and oppress the people.

I believe that most of the problems confronting Nigeria today are due to religious malpractices, and these errors cut across all the three major religions in the country. These religions have created a very toxic environment for Nigerians to coexist.

Heaven said so much about the false prophets and their victims, both willing and unwilling that we must admit that there are some true prophets of God in our society. Some prophets and preachers in the body of Christ can still hold on to the virtues that God expects of them.

Many are relatively unknown, as they are not as flamboyant and loud-mouthed as their false prophets' counterparts. Flamboyance and sincerity in the activities of God's vineyard can hardly go hand in hand. Looking through the Bible, no true prophet of God is described as flamboyant in dressing and social life.

However, some of these good prophets, too, struggle with some faults. While we are all humans and are fallible, with one or two areas of weakness we sometimes struggle with, it is not an excuse to dwell in sin. Some of these supposedly true prophets of God live not only in sin but seem comfortable in their state of moral bankruptcy.

Just as there are such prophets and men used by God in our churches today, so were some like that in the Bible.

Some biblical examples of men who identified with God but still displayed poor morals are as listed below:

1. King David.
2 Samuel 11:1-4 (KJV): And it came to pass, after the year was expired, at the time when kings go forth to battle, that David sent Joab, and his servants with him, and all Israel; and they destroyed the children of Ammon, and besieged Rabbah. But David tarried still at Jerusalem.

And it came to pass in an evening tide, that David arose from off his bed, and walked upon the roof of the king's house: and from the roof he saw a woman washing herself; and the woman was very beautiful to look upon.

And David sent and enquired after the woman. And one said, Is not this Bath-sheba, the daughter of Eliam, the wife of Uriah the Hittite?

And David sent messengers, and took her; and she came in unto him, and he lay with her; for she was purified from her uncleanness: and she returned unto her house.

When King David was supposed to be at the battleground, he was at home idle. He saw Bathsheba, the wife of one of his soldiers, and lusted after her. He ended up impregnating her, and to cover his wrongdoing; he ended up setting up Uriah, the husband of Bathsheba, to be killed.

David also displayed a spirit of unforgiveness until he was on his death bed. A man called Shimei cursed him when he was going into exile. When David returned from exile, Shimei came to him begging for forgiveness, and David swore to him that he would not be put to death. Then when he was to die, he recalled the deed of Shimei and instructed that he be killed even in his old age.

Curiously enough, this instruction for revenge were the last recorded words of King David on his death bed.

2 Samuel 16:5-10 (KJV): And when king David came to Bahurim, behold, thence came out a man of the family of the house of Saul, whose name was Shimei, the son of Gera: he came forth, and cursed still as he came.

And he cast stones at David, and at all the servants of king David: and all the people and all the mighty men were on his right hand and on his left.

And thus said Shimei when he cursed, Come out, come out, thou bloody man, and thou man of Belial:

The LORD hath returned upon thee all the blood of the house of Saul, in whose stead thou hast reigned; and the LORD hath delivered the kingdom into the hand of Absalom thy son: and, behold, thou art taken in thy mischief, because thou art a bloody man.

Then said Abishai the son of Zeruiah unto the king, Why

should this dead dog curse my Lord the king? let me go over, I pray thee, and take off his head.

And the king said, What have I to do with you, ye sons of Zeruiah? so let him curse, because the LORD hath said unto him, Curse David. Who shall then say, Wherefore hast thou done so?

2 Samuel 19:16, 18-20, 23 (KJV): And Shimei the son of Gera, a Benjamite, which was of Bahurim, hasted and came down with the men of Judah to meet king David.

And there went over a ferry boat to carry over the king's household, and to do what he thought good. And Shimei the son of Gera fell down before the king, as he was come over Jordan;

And said unto the king, Let not my Lord impute iniquity unto me, neither do thou remember that which thy servant did perversely the day that my Lord the king went out of Jerusalem, that the king should take it to his heart.

For thy servant doth know that I have sinned: therefore, behold, I am come the first this day of all the house of Joseph to go down to meet my Lord the king.

Therefore the king said unto Shimei, Thou shalt not die. And the king swore unto him.

In contrast to his words, David instructed his successor Solomon otherwise.

1 Kings 2:8-9 (KJV): And, behold, thou hast with thee Shimei the son of Gera, a Benjamite of Bahurim, which cursed me with a grievous curse in the day when I went to Mahanaim: but he came down to meet me at Jordan, and I sware to him by the LORD, saying, I will not put thee to death with the sword.

Now therefore hold him not guiltless: for thou art a wise man, and knowest what thou oughtest to do unto him; but his hoar head bring thou down to the grave with blood.

Solomon schemed the old man Shimei into a tight corner, restricting him from traveling outside Jerusalem all his days. Eventually, the inevitable happened, the now reasonably wealthy older man traveled outside of Jerusalem to bring back two of his servants who ran away from him.

Solomon heard and ordered that Shimei be killed. The details of this story can be found in *1 Kings 2: 36-46*.

2. King Solomon.
King Solomon enjoyed so much favor from God. He got the windfall of God's faithfulness to David, his father, and had no war all his days as King.

After he completed the temple building, God appeared to him and gave him mighty instructions that we still refer to.

2 Chronicles 7:13-14 (KJV): If I shut up heaven that there be no rain, or if I command the locusts to devour the land, or if I send pestilence among my people;

If my people, which are called by my name, shall humble

themselves, and pray, and seek my face, and turn from their wicked ways; then will I hear from heaven, and will forgive their sin, and will heal their land.

Unfortunately for King Solomon, however, despite enjoying so much favor from God and being blessed with wisdom, he still displayed some deplorable morals. He was not only instrumental in the killing of Shimei, but he also showed poor morals in marrying so many strange women. These strange women even turned his heart away from God.

1 Kings 11:1-8 (KJV): But king Solomon loved many strange women, together with the daughter of Pharaoh, women of the Moabites, Ammonites, Edomites, Zidonians, and Hittites;

Of the nations concerning which the LORD said unto the children of Israel, Ye shall not go in to them, neither shall they come in unto you: for surely they will turn away your heart after their gods: Solomon clave unto these in love.

And he had seven hundred wives, princesses, and three hundred concubines: and his wives turned away his heart.

For it came to pass, when Solomon was old, that his wives turned away his heart after other gods: and his heart was not perfect with the LORD his God, as was the heart of David his father.

For Solomon went after Ashtoreth the goddess of the Zidonians, and after Milcom the abomination of the Ammonites.

And Solomon did evil in the sight of the LORD, and went not fully after the LORD, as did David his father.

Then did Solomon build an high place for Chemosh, the abomination of Moab, in the hill that is before Jerusalem, and for Molech, the abomination of the children of Ammon.

And likewise, did he for all his strange wives, which burnt incense and sacrificed unto their gods.

King Solomon's case was a pathetic situation. After knowing God so closely and enjoying so much grace and favor from Him, he still displayed some level of moral decadence unbecoming of a child of God.

3. Samson.
Samson is another case that puts a question mark on the saying of *Romans 11:29 (KJV): For the gifts and calling of God are without repentance.* Despite his persistence in making all the possible wrong decisions, Samson succeeded but still enjoyed the grace of God till his death.

Twice he married wrongly. He did one of the most extraordinary, recorded deeds: removing the city gate and carrying it to a mountain top; scripture recorded that he was coming from the place of a prostitute where he spent the night.

Despite his peculiar gift, Samson was never an excellent example of a true child of God.

Judges 14:1-3 (KJV): And Samson went down to Timnath, and saw a woman in Timnath of the daughters of the Philistines.

And he came up, and told his father and his mother, and said, I have seen a woman in Timnath of the daughters of the Philistines: now therefore get her for me as wife.

Then his father and his mother said unto him, Is there never a woman among the daughters of thy brethren, or among all my people, that thou goest to take a wife of the uncircumcised Philistines? And Samson said unto his father, Get her for me; for she pleaseth me well.

Judges 16:1-3 (KJV): Then went Samson to Gaza, and saw there an harlot, and went in unto her.

And it was told the Gazites, saying, Samson is come hither. And they compassed him in, and laid wait for him all night in the gate of the city, and were quiet all the night, saying, In the morning, when it is day, we shall kill him.

And Samson lay till midnight, and arose at midnight, and took the doors of the gate of the city, and the two posts, and went away with them, bar and all, and put them upon his shoulders, and carried them up to the top of a hill that is before Hebron.

4. Gehazi.

Gehazi is another terrible example of a man who had all the opportunity to attain legendary status with God but fluffed the line with moral bankruptcy. He could have succeeded Prophet Elisha and probably gotten twice the power of God on Elisha, which is four times the power of God on Elijah. He, however, lost it over some filthy lucre.

1 Peter 5:2 (KJV): Feed the flock of God which is among you, taking the oversight thereof, not by constraint, but willingly; not for filthy lucre, but of a ready mind.

Gehazi was given to filthy lucre, and it destroyed his ministry so early.

2 Kings 5:20-24 (KJV): But Gehazi, the servant of Elisha the man of God, said, Behold, my master hath spared Naaman this Syrian, in not receiving at his hands that which he brought: but, as the LORD liveth, I will run after him, and take somewhat of him.

So Gehazi followed after Naaman. And when Naaman saw him running after him, he lighted down from the chariot to meet him, and said, Is all well?

And he said All is well. My master hath sent me, saying, Behold, even now there be come to me from mount Ephraim two young men of the sons of the prophets: give them, I pray thee, a talent of silver, and two changes of garments.

And Naaman said, Be content, take two talents. And he urged him, and bound two talents of silver in two bags, with two changes of garments, and laid them upon two of his servants; and they bare them before him.

And when he came to the tower, he took them from their hand, and bestowed them in the house: and he let the men go, and they departed.

Not all moral issue has to do with fornication and adultery. Stealing and obtaining gifts by fraudulent means are ethical decadence issues too.

5. Prophet Elisha

Another person to look at is Prophet Elisha. He was a firebrand prophet of God who wrought many miracles in his time. However, he too displayed a form of moral weakness in committing multiple murders of some children, forty-two of them in all!

One puzzling detail of his story, just like Samson's, is that he carried out his wrong action just after performing one of his greatest miracles of healing the land of Jericho.

2 Kings 2:22-24 (KJV): So the waters were healed unto this day, according to the saying of Elisha which he spake.

And he went up from thence unto Bethel: and as he was going up by the way, there came forth little children out of the city, and mocked him, and said unto him, Go up, thou bald head; go up, thou bald head.

And he turned back, and looked on them, and cursed them in the name of the LORD. And there came forth two she bears out of the wood, and tare forty and two children of them.

Just as some prophets of God and men close to the heart of God abused privilege in the days of old, many are doing the same today. Most of the men of the days of old probably made peace with God after their wrong acts, but we see many modern-day prophets rejoicing in their follies.

Falling into sin is not what destroys a man but remaining in the dirty gutters of such sin. *Proverbs 24:16 (KJV) says: For a just man falleth seven times, and riseth up again: but the wicked shall fall into mischief.* The Bible still refers to such a person as a just man despite the falls.

Many men of God who started well are gradually slipping into the mess of sin without care. They believe the grace of God on them is enough, but *God is not mocked, whatever a man sows he shall reap (Galatians 6:7).*

Many careless pastors unwittingly send many men to hell with wrong counsel and show bad examples. Some are genuinely gifted but have a hidden second wife. Some are genuinely favored with unusual talents but are given to greed and filthy lucre. And some who, being mightily used of God, still struggle with their temperament.

The good news is that there is still an opportunity to deal with these areas of weakness and walk perfectly before God. There is no weakness of man that God cannot deal with if only the one suffering from this weakness will admit that they need help.

The Bible says in the gospel according to *Matthew 5:48 (KJV): Be ye therefore perfect, even as your Father which is in heaven is perfect.* This means perfection is a possibility.

May you find perfection in your walk with God. May you become all you can become for Him, in Jesus' name.

Chapter Eleven

Turn Your Eyes Upon Jesus

Numbers 21:5-9 (KJV): And the people spake against God, and against Moses, Wherefore have ye brought us up out of Egypt to die in the wilderness? for there is no bread, neither is there any water; and our soul loatheth this light bread.
And the LORD sent fiery serpents among the people, and they bit the people; and much people of Israel died.
Therefore the people came to Moses, and said, We have sinned, for we have spoken against the LORD, and against thee; pray unto the LORD, that he take away the serpents from us. And Moses prayed for the people.
And the LORD said unto Moses, Make thee a fiery serpent, and set it upon a pole: and it shall come to pass, that every one that is bitten, when he looketh upon it, shall live.
And Moses made a serpent of brass, and put it upon a pole, and it came to pass, that if a serpent had bitten any man, when he beheld the serpent of brass, he lived.

1. *O soul are you weary and troubled*
   No light in the darkness you see
   There's light for a look at the Savior
   And life more abundant and free

   Chorus:
   Turn your eyes upon Jesus
   Look full in His wonderful face
   And the things of life will grow strangely dim
   In the light of His glory and grace.

2. *From death to life everlasting*
   He rose, and we followed Him there
   O'er us death no longer have dominion
   For more than conquerors are we

   Chorus:
   Turn your eyes upon Jesus
   Look full in His wonderful face
   And the things of life will grow strangely dim
   In the light of His glory and grace..

Just as man needed to be saved from Satan, the serpent, the Israelites needed to be saved from the snakes in the wilderness. A snake is a symbol of poison or venom, and so was religion, a symbol of reward or punishment in the Old Testament. However, in the case of the venom-less brass snake, it had no poison. It has an outward look of danger but has no venom. So does Jesus and His teaching. There is a fear of going to hell at the back of the mind of some who hear and accept the gospel. However, men going to hell is never the will of God for any man.

At the beginning of the chapter, the hymn admonished that when we find ourselves struggling in darkness, we should turn our focus upon Jesus. It further tells us the ageless truth: The more you focus on Jesus, the less the significance of your challenge.

The second stanza maintained that by turning our focus on Jesus, we rise from a state of spiritual death to life everlasting. As a result, death will no longer have dominion over us. It pays to focus on Jesus. No wonder another hymn starts with the line "Tis so sweet to trust in Jesus..."

One wonderful thing about focusing on Jesus is that you will never be put to shame. In other words, you will never be disappointed.

They looked unto him, and were lightened: and their faces were not ashamed. Psalms 34:5 (KJV)

The above quotation from the Bible captures the explanation above so beautifully. Looking unto Jesus and focusing on Him brings enlightenment. Focusing on Him brings fresh ideas, understanding, and solutions to our challenges. New King James Version of *Psalms 34:5* says: *They looked to Him and were radiant, and their faces were not ashamed.*

Radiance suggests illumination, or fluorescing, which means to give light. Those who look up to Christ can become so enlightened that their brightness influences others around them. It pays to focus on Him.

There are several other reasons we should always focus on God through Christ. Some of these reasons are as follows.

1. God is our creator.
Genesis 1:1 (KJV) says: In the beginning, God created the heavens and the earth.

2. There is no other route to true salvation.
John 14:6 (KJV) says: Jesus saith unto him, I am the way, the truth, and the life: no man cometh unto the Father, but by me.

3. Only Him can forgive us of our sins.
2 Chronicles 7:14 (KJV): If my people, which are called by my name, shall humble themselves, and pray, and seek my face, and turn from their wicked ways; then will I hear from heaven, and will forgive their sin, and will heal their land.

4. He can sanctify us.
Ezekiel 20:12 (KJV) says: Moreover also I gave them my sabbaths, to be a sign between me and them, that they might know that I am the LORD that sanctifies them.

5. Healing comes from Him
Jeremiah 30:17a (KJV): For I will restore health unto thee, and I will heal thee of thy wounds, saith the LORD.

6. Protection is certain in Him
David said when forced into exile in *Psalms 3:3 (KJV): But thou, O LORD, art a shield for me; my glory, and the lifter up of mine head.*

God is indeed able to be a shield about us just as he shields

Jerusalem and His people of old (Psalms 125:2).

7. He blesses without adding sorrow.
Proverbs 10:22 (KJV): The blessing of the LORD, it maketh rich, and he addeth no sorrow with it.

There are several other reasons why we should focus our attention on Him. For instance, in 1 Samuel from chapter one, Hannah, who had no child, focused her attention on God and her case turned for the better.

When faced with imminent destruction, the children of Israel called on God with their full attention and focus, and God did not fail them for once.

Hebrews 12:2 (KJV) clearly say: *Looking unto Jesus the author and finisher of our faith; who for the joy that was set before him endured the cross, despising the shame, and is set down at the right hand of the throne of God.* It is the divine will of God that we focus our attention on God through Jesus Christ, the author and finisher of our faith.

However, it is interesting that many people do not understand how to focus on God. Some think it is about staring at the picture of Christ on the cross or reverencing His statue. Looking unto God, focusing on Him through our Lord Jesus Christ is more than that. In my opinion, making statute for God is an idolatrous practice; He is a spirit and should be worshiped in truth and spirit, Exodus 20:4 and John 4:24.

There are several ways we can focus on God. This is not to say that these ways are options, as we are supposed to

focus on Him using as many of the ways as possible.

1. Tarrying in His presence.
Psalms 27:14 (KJV): Wait on the LORD: be of good courage, and he shall strengthen thine heart: wait, I say, on the LORD.

2. Be constantly aware of Him and be prayerful.
Romans 12:11-12 (KJV): Not slothful in business; fervent in spirit; serving the Lord; Rejoicing in hope; patient in tribulation; continuing instant in prayer;

3. Meditating on His word.
2 Timothy 2:15 (KJV): Study to shew thyself approved unto God, a workman that needeth not to be ashamed, rightly dividing the word of truth.

4. Consciously doing His will.
Matthew 6:10 (KJV): Thy kingdom come. Thy will be done in earth, as it is in heaven.

5. By always praising Him.
Psalms 22:3 (KJV): But thou art holy, O thou that inhabitest the praises of Israel.

6. By worshiping Him.
Romans 12:1 (NIV): Therefore, I urge you brothers, in view of God's mercy, to offer yourself as living sacrifices, holy and pleasing to God- this is your spiritual act of worship.

7. By taking your challenges to Him
Matthew 11:28 (KJV): Come unto me, all ye that labor and are heavy laden, and I will give you rest.

8. By preaching the gospel constantly.
2 Timothy 4:2 (KJV): Preach the word; be instant in season, out of season; reprove, rebuke, exhort with all longsuffering and doctrine.

Despite focusing on Him, there are situations in life when God is silent. There are cases when it seems as if God is not available to listen to our prayers. There are, however, many reasons why God permits such experience. As Christians, we all need the wilderness experience in walking with God. A period when you are separated from God to go through certain life-changing experiences. Jesus Christ had a wilderness experience. David, too, had a wilderness experience, and Joseph and all the prominent prophets in the Bible. The wilderness experience is part of our Christian race.

Some reasons why God goes silent on us include the following listed below but are not limited to these;

1. Test time.

It could be a time for us to be tested to merit the next level.

But the God of all grace, who hath called us unto his eternal glory by Christ Jesus, after that ye have suffered a while, make you perfect, stablish, strengthen, settle you. 1 Peter 5: 10 (KJV).

2. When you ask amiss.
We often make the mistake of asking the wrong question

or making the wrong requests. At such times, God may not answer and not correct us immediately, especially when such error is below our expected level of maturity in Christ.

Ye ask, and receive not, because ye ask amiss, that ye may consume it upon your lusts. James 4: 3 (KJV).

3. God is speaking, but you are not listening.
There are situations when God speaks to us, but we are too distracted by the flesh to hear Him. He may speak through signs and dreams, but we keep missing the message. The ability to hear from Him significantly differentiates spiritual men from carnal men.

But the natural man receiveth not the things of the Spirit of God: for they are foolishness unto him: neither can he know them, because they are spiritually discerned.

But he that is spiritual judgeth all things, yet he himself is judged of no man. 1 Corinthians 2: 14-15 (KJV).

4. It could be to make you stronger.
Momentary wilderness experience helps us to be stronger. It gives us more confidence when we have survived the times of trials and tribulations. Many who pass through difficult experiences return better with a better positive influence on the world around them. Such incidents often precede manifestation, as it is the period of preparation. It is a necessity for spiritual growth for every child of God.

For I reckon that the sufferings of this present time are not worthy to be compared with the glory which shall be revealed in us. For the earnest expectation of the creature waiteth for the manifestation of the sons of God. Romans 8: 18-19 (KJV).

5. Your glory is near.
As earlier said, passing through a wilderness experience prepares you for the assignment ahead, leading to your manifestation to the world. It is also an experience that ushers us into our glory. As a child of God, such periods should be wished for or expected for the same reason above. When you identify a particular experience as a wilderness experience, persevere and rejoice, for your glory is around the corner. May your glorification be eternal in Jesus' name.

For our light affliction, which is but for a moment, worketh for us a far more exceeding and eternal weight of glory. 2 Corinthians 4: 17 (KJV).

6. God is giving you a testimony for future reference.
Our wilderness experience, at times, is testimony for future reference. It may be God's sign of goodness to a child of God to shame his enemies or confirm him as a true child of God. David said in *Psalms 23:4* that *though I walk through the valley of the shadow of death, I will fear no evil: for thou art with me; thy rod and thy staff they comfort me.* He has survived the valley of the shadow of death before, so he can safely not fear.

The rod and staff referred to here are not always palatable. While the staff is to direct, the rod is to correct with blows. It is not enjoyable when we go through it, but we look back with appreciation when we come out of it. It is God's sign of goodness to His children.

Shew me a token for good; that they which hate me may see it, and be ashamed: because thou, LORD, hast holpen me, and comforted me. Psalms 86:17 (KJV).

7. It could be due to demonic restriction.
We are not ignorant of the devices of the devil (*2 Corinthians 2:11*). God can answer our prayers, but the manifestation tarries because of demonic restrictions. We erroneously think it is God withholding an answer to our request, but in the real sense, it is not so.

Daniel prayed in the Bible, and God answered his prayer. Unfortunately, a demon in charge of Persia where he was, prevented the response to his request from getting to him. The angel bringing his answer was held up for twenty-one days by this demon until angel Michael came to his rescue. We should know that twenty-one days may sometimes turn into twenty-one years. That is why we should pray without ceasing even when we are not getting the response we need (*1 Thessalonians 5: 17*). And if such a person expecting an answer to prayer should lose hope and stop praying, such a response may never come. We need to pray fervently concerning all things, either with or without manifesting the answers to our prayers.

And he said unto me, O Daniel, a man greatly beloved, understand the words that I speak unto thee, and stand upright: for unto thee am I now sent. And when he had spoken this word unto me, I stood trembling.

Then said he unto me, Fear not, Daniel: for from the first day that thou didst set thine heart to understand, and to chasten thyself before thy God, thy words were heard, and I am come for thy words.

But the prince of the kingdom of Persia withstood me one and twenty days: but, lo, Michael, one of the chief princes, came to help me; and I remained there with the kings of Persia. Daniel 10: 11-13 (KJV).

These are just a few of the situations leading to a wilderness experience. There are so many others not mentioned above; for instance, a wilderness experience could be God keeping you away from the danger of your enemies whom you might not be able to handle. It could also be due to God helping to protect your already given testimony to fullness. A wilderness experience could also be for humbling and correction. King Nebuchadnezzar can tell us a thing or two about that.

A wilderness experience should be endured and maximized. Once we are sure it is not a case of demonic restriction or even demonic oppression, we should embrace and maximize such periods.

How do we maximize our wilderness experience? This is a fundamental question every Christian should ask and find answers to. It is not enough to pass through such experience; it should be maximized. As a matter of principle, a child of God must be able to discern why he must go through certain dry patches in life and then know how to manage such situations better.

Some men have been caused to be thrown in prison so they can be separated from the outside world and left with nothing to read but the Bible. That way, they met God, and their lives changed forever. Maximize your wilderness period. Make the best of your separation experience. There is no better personality to be with at such a time than God. Hence, the answer to maximizing our wilderness experience is simple: Stay focused on God through Jesus Christ.

In *Acts 4:12 (KJV)*: *Neither is there salvation in any other: for there is none other name under heaven given among men, whereby we must be saved.*

That explains the name to hold on to during our dry period in walking with God. The name guarantees salvation and a positive outcome for every unsavory situation.

When Paul and Silas were in prison, they knew what name to call on in prayer; they knew which God to turn to and ask for help.

And at midnight, Paul and Silas prayed, and sang praises unto God: and the prisoners heard them.

And suddenly there was a great earthquake, so that the foundations of the prison were shaken: and immediately all the doors were opened, and every one's bands were loosed. Acts 16: 25-26 (KJV).

They came out of the ordeal smiling in victory at the end of the day. Those men knew what to do when passing through an unpleasant situation.

David is another interesting example. He composed several songs during his wilderness experience days, which are still references for praise and worship in Christianity today. He managed his wilderness experience perfectly well.

It is a grave mistake to involve others who are not of discerning hearts in our wilderness experience. Often, such experience draws us away from the noise of carnality and helps us focus on God. But we at times still carry necessary baggage with us.

God did not instruct Abraham to take Lot along when he was called out from his kindreds. That decision almost scuttled his destiny and purpose in life in more than one way.

When Job passed through his own wilderness experience, he also made the mistake of confiding in his friends. If you follow the account well in the book of Job, you sense that because of the accusations from his three friends, Job's faith had begun to fail when God appeared to him to save his tattered faith from shredding to bits would have made him lose all.

Your wilderness experience is for you; enjoy it while it lasts. The fewer the people you involve, the better the chance of coming out smiling. Some people begin to go from one pastor to another and compound their problems. Some begin to question God, further slowing down the process the experience is meant to teach. Some even outrightly curse God, as Mrs. Job advised her husband. The result of cursing God, rebelling against Him, or running after other gods in your wilderness experience is to be cut off. Such a person is cut off from God, which is worse.

Another critical point to note when passing through a wilderness experience is staying focused and not allowing any distraction. Distraction in this situation will lead you to seek an alternative to God. Imagine Job going to prayer houses and herbalists for a solution to his problem. He would only add to his suffering and may even lose his soul. Earlier, we looked at *Jeremiah 2:13*, where we read that these deities are broken cisterns that cannot help, especially if the hardship or the predicament is from God. Who is man to force the hand of God? Especially a man relying on diabolic means.

In *1 Samuel 28: 3-25*, Saul sought after a witch in Endor. It was God who rejected him from being king; who is a witch to help him? Even when the witch summoned the spirit of Samuel, it was a futile effort. God was the one who rejected Saul; how can Samuel be the solution to such a troubling situation?

The answer Samuel gave Saul says it all.

And Samuel said to Saul, Why hast thou disquieted me, to bring me up? And Saul answered, I am sore distressed; for the Philistines make war against me, and God is departed from me, and answereth me no more, neither by prophets nor by dreams: therefore I have called thee, that thou mayest make known unto me what I shall do.

Then said Samuel, Wherefore then dost thou ask of me, seeing the LORD is departed from thee, and is become thine enemy?

And the LORD hath done to him, as he spake by me: for the LORD hath rent the kingdom out of thine hand, and given it to thy neighbor, even to David:

Because thou obeyedst not the voice of the LORD, nor executedst his fierce wrath upon Amalek, therefore hath the LORD done this thing unto thee this day.

Moreover the LORD will also deliver Israel with thee into the hand of the Philistines: and to morrow shalt thou and thy sons be with me: the LORD also shall deliver the host of Israel into the hand of the Philistines.

Then Saul fell straightway all along on the earth, and was sore afraid, because of the words of Samuel: and there was no strength in him; for he had eaten no bread all the day, nor all the night. 1 Samuel 28: 15-20 (KJV).

The truth is, it would be better not to have known God than to know Him and throw it all away because of a brief dry patch.

2 Peter 2:21-22 (KJV) says: *For it had been better for them not to have known the way of righteousness, than, after they have known it, to turn from the holy commandment delivered unto them.*

But it is happened unto them according to the true proverb; the dog is turned to his own vomit again; and the sow that was washed to her wallowing in the mire.

No matter how bad the situation may be, or how dark the cloud over your heart may be, no matter how hopeless the condition, trust God and remain focused on Him through our Lord Jesus Christ. No one who toed this path has ever regretted it; you can never be the exception. Endure your wilderness experience and be eased into your glory in Jesus' name.

Chapter Twelve

The Simplicity of the Gospel of Christ

And he said unto them, Go ye into all the world, and preach the gospel to every creature.
He that believeth and is baptized shall be saved, but he that believeth not shall be damned.
And these signs shall follow them that believe; In my name shall they cast out devils; they shall speak with new tongues;
They shall take up serpents; and if they drink any deadly thing, it shall not hurt them; they shall lay hands on the sick, and they shall recover.
So then after the Lord had spoken unto them, he was received up into heaven and sat on the right hand of God.
And they went forth, and preached everywhere, the Lord working with them, and confirming the word with signs following. Amen.
Mark 16: 15-20 (KJV).

n the account above, Jesus Christ addressed His disciples for the last time in the flesh before He was caught up in heaven. His last address is a commandment to His disciple to evangelize to the entire world. If His last address was on evangelism, then, needless to say, evangelism must be significant to Him.

Jesus Christ, in this address, was able to express both the simplicity and complexity of evangelism at the same time. He covered the extremes of evangelism in more than one way. For instance, He mentioned preaching to the entire world, which is general. Then to every creature, that is personal. He said those who believe shall be saved, and those who reject the message of the cross shall be damned. That is yet another pair of extremes covered.

Then Jesus made His disciples know that no harm can come to them while evangelizing, which is very soothing to know. Also, while they will not be harmed, they are empowered to liberate those in all types of bondage by just laying their hands on them. That is yet another pair of extremes covered.

It is interesting to know that a good understanding of evangelizing the gospel of Christ can help Christians not fall victim to false prophets' hands. The more you understand the gospel, the more you see the difference between the practice of a false prophet and what a model man of God ought to be.

The message of the gospel may seem complex, but the more we understand it, the easier it becomes. The gospel can be as easy as "Give your life to Jesus, love God, love others, and love yourself."

A group of youths traveled for a Christian program in a coaster bus. Since the journey took a few hours, their coordinators randomly picked some to preach on the bus, giving each preacher a few minutes.

They all preached, each trying to display their knowledge of the Bible as should be expected among such young and ambitious people. Several years on, the topics they preached and the Bible verses they quoted have been forgotten except for the unique message of one of them that stood the test of time in the mind of all present.

Why was the message unique? It was because of the simplicity. The young man, when he was called on to preach, panicked. A few people from his parish giggled, knowing he was not literate and shy. After the coordinator forced him to preach for about fifteen minutes, he kept repeating, "Give your life to Jesus; His second coming is near. Give your life to Jesus."

Many of the youths in that bus laughed at him, but over twenty years on, the complex messages delivered by the other preachers have been forgotten. However, the simple sermon of that uneducated shy young man remained in the head of all present for years.

The second stanza of a popular Christian song goes thus:

If you can't pray like Peter
If you can't preach like Paul
Just tell the love of Jesus

And say He died for all.

The power of the gospel of Christ is not about plenty of words but in the grace of God that rests on the process.

What then is the Gospel of Christ?

The gospel means good news, while evangelism means to proclaim abroad. Therefore, the Gospel of Christ is simply the good news about Christ. What is the good news about Christ? The good news about Christ is *John 3:16-18 (KJV): For God so loved the world, that he gave his only begotten Son, that whosoever believeth in him should not perish, but have everlasting life.*

For God sent not his Son into the world to condemn the world; but that the world through him might be saved.

He that believeth in him is not condemned: but he that believeth not is condemned already because he hath not believed in the name of the only begotten Son of God.

What is the good news about Jesus Christ? The good news about Jesus Christ is *John 14:6 (KJV): Jesus saith unto him, I am the way, the truth, and the life: no man cometh unto the Father, but by me.*

What is the good news about Jesus Christ? The good news about Jesus is *Acts 4:12 (KJV): Neither is there salvation in any other: for there is none other name under heaven given among men, whereby we must be saved.*

The Gospel is not entirely a New Testament affair. The root of the gospel can be traced to the Old Testament. The essence of the gospel can be traced as far back as the days of Moses in the book of Numbers.

Numbers 14:21 (KJV) says: But as truly as I live, all the earth shall be filled with the glory of the LORD.

There was a need for the world to be filled with the glory of God. Jesus Christ was God in human form. After His short stay on earth, there was a need for this glory to spread abroad, hence the need for evangelism.

In the book of *Isaiah 11:9 (KJV)*, the Bible says: *They shall not hurt nor destroy in all my holy mountain: for the earth shall be full of the knowledge of the LORD, as the waters cover the sea.*

Here, the prophet Isaiah spoke about a prophecy that the earth would be filled with the knowledge of the Lord as the waters cover the sea. How will this knowledge of the Lord go round the world? Evangelism. What is this knowledge of the Lord? The gospel of God in human form; that is, Jesus Christ.

Habakkuk 2:14 (KJV) puts everything involved in evangelism and the Gospel of Christ from the Old Testament into better perspective. The prophet Habakkuk says: *For the earth shall be filled with the knowledge of the glory of the LORD, as the waters cover the sea.*

He prophesied from his era that a time would come when the world shall be filled with the knowledge of the glory of God.

You will begin to appreciate the enormity of this prophecy after all these years if you consider that up till today, the world is still not filled with the knowledge of Jehovah, the only true God.

The above analysis showed that the coming of Jesus Christ to the world was a part of a process. It was not an isolated event but a continuation of a process that began long ago.

For the good news about the benevolence and love of God the Father to go round the world, giving the world a chance for repentance, men will have to take the news to the uttermost end of the world. God added more importance to the equation by saying that the end of the earth shall not come until the Gospel of God in human form is preached to the entire world.

Matthew 24:14 (KJV) says: And this gospel of the kingdom shall be preached in all the world for a witness unto all nations; and then shall the end come.

For men to take this good news to the uttermost part of the earth, God himself had to come in the form of man through God the Son to show the elected men how to get the job done. Not only that, in several portions of the Old Testament, prophesies were given about the coming of Jesus Christ. He was not just to come and tell stories of the good news; instead, He demonstrated the good news by dying for our sins.

But God commendeth his love toward us, in that, while we were yet sinners, Christ died for us. Romans 5:8(KJV).

We love him because he first loved us. 1 John 4:19 (KJV).

Some Old Testament prophesies about the coming of Christ were so detailed that we cannot but keep referring to them. For instance, *Isaiah 9:6-7 (KJV)* was so detailed in the account of the Prophet Isaiah. It says*: For unto us a child is born, unto us a son is given: and the government shall be upon his shoulder: and his name shall be called Wonderful, Counsellor, The mighty God, The everlasting Father, The Prince of Peace.*

Of the increase of his government and peace there shall be no end, upon the throne of David, and upon his kingdom, to order it, and to establish it with judgment and with justice from henceforth even forever. The zeal of the LORD of hosts will perform this.

The foundation of the gospel of Christ was laid long before the New Testament era. Despite the seeming complexity of the gospel and the length of years spent laying the foundation for the actualization of this gospel by the coming of Jesus Christ, the gospel itself is straightforward. Apart from the above, the gospel can still be as simple as "God is love." We can infer that all Jesus came to do can be summarized into those three words, "God is love."

As noted earlier, just as the Gospel can be simple, so can evangelism of the Gospel. There are two sides to evangelism. There is the physical side and the deeper spiritual side. Physical evangelism can be about telling the world about the love and essence of the coming of Jesus Christ. Spiritual evangelism has to do with the process and effort of wrestling the souls of the lost from the claws of the devil and his demons.

Why then do we need to spread this gospel around the world? Why should this message of love be preached to every creature of the world?

1. Christ commands it.
Jesus said unto him, Let the dead bury their dead: but go thou and preach the kingdom of God. Luke 9:60 (KJV).

2. The whole earth must hear the good news before the end can come.
And this gospel of the kingdom shall be preached in all the world for a witness unto all nations; and then shall the end come. Matthew 24:14 (KJV).

3. It is the power of God unto salvation.
For I am not ashamed of the gospel of Christ: for it is the power of God unto salvation to everyone that believeth; to the Jew first, and also to the Greek. Romans 1:16 (KJV).

4. It is the wise thing to do.
The fruit of the righteous is a tree of life, and he that winneth souls is wise. Proverbs 11:30 (KJV).

5. It attracts the glory of God.
And they that be wise shall shine as the brightness of the firmament; and they that turn many to righteousness as the stars forever and ever. Daniel 12:3 (KJV).

6. More laborers are needed to spread the good news.
Then saith he unto his disciples, The harvest truly is plenteous, but the laborers are few;

Pray ye therefore the Lord of the harvest, that he will send forth laborers into his harvest. Matthew 9:37-38 (KJV).

7. Not sharing the gospel is selfishness.
Matthew 22:37-39 (KJV): Jesus said unto him, Thou shalt love the Lord thy God with all thy heart, and with all thy soul, and with all thy mind. This is the first and great commandment. And the second is like unto it, Thou shalt love thy neighbor as thyself.

The subject of the Gospel of Christ is an integral part of human existence and when the expected end time shall come. The importance of the Gospel of Christ cannot be overemphasized. There are different simple ways of spreading the Gospel of love. There are various simple ways of making the world around us know about the glorious Gospel of Christ. While the old practices are still acceptable, modern technology has provided several new options for sharing the Gospel.

Oral: This is the oldest means of sharing the good news. It involves speaking to others about the Gospel. It is still the most practical way and how most allow for feedback, primarily unconscious feedback, from the person listening to the Gospel. It could be through one-to-one evangelism, morning cry, or public place preaching.

Written: This too is quite old. Most of the books of the New Testament are products of written evangelism. It can be through letter-writing, pamphlets, bulletins, books, etc.

Online: Social media usage has dramatically improved the level of communication and the possibility of evangelism.

Social media like Facebook, TikTok, WhatsApp, Instagram, and others offer some form of evangelism unavailable some years ago.

Several other evangelizing forms include music, drama, behavior, giving, welfare outreach, media outreach, etc. They are making the spread of the Gospel easy.

One crucial factor in making the spread of the Gospel easier is Power! Jesus Christ also imparted on His disciples, instructed them not to go out to evangelize until they are endued with power from above through the Holy Spirit.

Then opened their understanding so that they might understand the scriptures,

And ye are witnesses of these things.

And, behold, I send the promise of my Father upon you: but tarry ye in the city of Jerusalem, until ye be endued with power from on high. Luke 24:45, 48-49 (KJV).

But ye shall receive power, after that the Holy Ghost is come upon you: and ye shall be witnesses unto me both in Jerusalem, and in all Judaea, and in Samaria, and unto the uttermost part of the earth. Acts 1:8 (KJV).

With the empowerment of the Holy Spirit, the simplicity of the gospel and the ease of spreading it abroad becomes clearer. Another essential preparatory factor to make carrying the gospel easy is Prayer. After adequate prayer, you are charged up enough to withstand every demonic agent of obstruction to the work of God through you.

But we will give ourselves continually to prayer and the ministry of the word. Acts 6:4 (KJV).

A third point to note before venturing out to spread the knowledge of the glory of God is His presence. You must carry His presence with you spiritually wherever you go.

Who also hath made us able ministers of the New Testament; not of the letter, but the spirit: for the letter killeth, but the spirit giveth life. *2 Corinthians 3:6 (KJV).*

It is the spirit that quickeneth; the flesh profiteth nothing: the words that I speak unto you, they are spirit, and they are life. John 6:63 (KJV).

Many of us struggle unnecessarily when we evangelize. We put in too much energy and intellect, thinking it is the way to get the job done. One little detail we forget is that when we evangelize, we are not the ones doing the work. The Holy Spirit does His will through the vessel we make available. All we must do is be available, be prayerful and then get out of the way of the Holy Spirit and allow Him to take control.

If you go out in His strength, the Holy Spirit will be with you. Jesus Christ promised to be with us to the end of the world.

Teaching them to observe all things whatsoever I have commanded you: and, lo, I am with you always, even unto the end of the world. Amen. Matthew 28;20 (KJV).

Another essential fact about evangelizing is that it is good to go in a group of at least two. There are several reasons for this. One of the reasons for group rather than individual evangelism is that both aspects of evangelism must be covered simultaneously. Both the physical and the spiritual aspects must be given attention. When we share the gospel with someone, and he refuses, it could be that a demon whispers into his ears not to listen as we speak to the person. So, while one person is ministering to a targeted soul, the other person should be praying in the Spirit against such a demon manipulating the mind of the targeted soul.

Finally, one brilliant thing evangelism also offers the person evangelizing is a constant visit to the basics of Christianity. Such basic facts as Christ's love are revisited and the need to be born again. Other basic knowledge in faith and belief will also come up for consideration.

This basic knowledge of Christianity reminds a true child of God of what he stands for. Also, it helps to differentiate between a true man of God and a counterfeit man of God. The more we compare the life and ministry of all the teeming false prophets to the basic teachings of Christ, the more the likelihood of seeing through their lies and not falling for their antics.

The ministry of reconciliation through basic evangelism is the way to go. Taking the Gospel of love and grace to other people helps you be better rooted in Christ Jesus and protects you from the false prophets and false teachers.

Chapter Thirteen

Laziness Knows Them by Name

*Give not sleep to thine eyes, nor slumber to thine eyelids.
Deliver thyself as a roe from the hand of the hunter, and as a bird from the hand of the fowler.
Go to the ant, thou sluggard; consider her ways, and be wise:
Which having no guide, overseer, or ruler,
Provideth her meat in the summer, and gathereth her food in the harvest.
How long wilt thou sleep, O sluggard? when wilt thou arise out of thy sleep?
Yet a little sleep, a little slumber, a little folding of the hands to sleep:
So shall thy poverty come as one that travelleth, and thy want as an armed man.
Proverbs 6: 4-11 (KJV).*

Laziness is a trait that is gradually creeping into Christian practice today. Several things that the pioneers held dear has now been systematically watered down. From firm doctrine to behavioral discipline, watering down to accommodate the spreading laziness seems the order of the day.

The Bible passage above aptly captures the situation of Christianity in our modern age. Before the Bible can say give not your eyes to sleep, it suggests that a person must have been sleeping a lot. The following verse hints that by being alert, one can effectively protect or deliver oneself from the hands of hunters and fowlers after one's life and freedom. It is true about our situation today because the devil has been tormenting some Christians because they sleep too much.

A Christian who cannot miss his sleep for prayer is not ready for spiritual warfare. A prayerless Christian is a powerless Christian. Every Christian who prays but cannot tarry with God in the place of earnest prayer will always have a delay in the delivery of his expectations. Prayer in place of sleep is essential for victory and deliverance in Christianity.

And at midnight Paul and Silas prayed, and sang praises unto God: and the prisoners heard them.

And suddenly there was a great earthquake so that the foundations of the prison were shaken: and immediately all the doors were opened, and everyone's bands were loosed. Acts 16: 25-26 (KJV).

Note, it was not the prayer Paul and Silas prayed in the

daytime that made the difference in their situation but the prayer they prayed in the middle of the night. Midnight is when one is most likely to be asleep; midnight is when the powers of wickedness are most active. Midnight is when evil seeds are put down in the lives of men as they sleep.

Another parable put he forth unto them, saying, The kingdom of heaven is likened unto a man which sowed good seed in his field:

But while men slept, his enemy came and sowed tares among the wheat, and went his way. Matthew 13: 24-35 (KJV).

Give not your eyes to sleep always. Do not spend all night sleeping as a child of God.

Verse 6 asked that the person the text is addressed should go to the ant and learn her ways and thereby receive wisdom. Ants are busy, hardworking insects who work hard during the dry season to gather all the food they eat during the cold or wet season. They are strong and can carry far more objects than their body size. If ants are working hard, the same cannot be said of our modern-day Christians. Special mention must be made of the new generation of Christians.

The text finished with comparisons of the lazy man to certain life events. A lazy man's lot is similar to a man who traveled to a far away land and squandered all his money. Such a careless man will return to poverty. When armed men attack a poor and weak man, they can take away all he has, and he will be left with nothing. In this regard, he is not far different from a lazy man who will not work to earn money or improve his life.

The new age is rife with the spirit of laziness. In our society today, modern technologies and robots are fast taking away physical activities from us. As a result, more people come down with cardiovascular and cardiopulmonary complications like high blood pressure and respiratory complications.

The remote control is now available rather than getting off the sofa to change the television channel. Rather than go out to the field to watch a football game, you can now sit on a chair at home and watch live matches anywhere in the world.

Also, people used to see their friends and spend time together. Today, people now have virtual friends on social media and can spend all day chatting online without knowing the people. We hear of cases where people who decide to meet virtual friends lose their lives to the evil friends they had kept on the internet for some time.

Several years ago, traveling or going out meant walking. Even where horses are available, riding a horse still requires a level of fitness. Riding a horse is exercise. These days, however, there are so many traveling options with varying elevated levels of relative efficiency. A business trip that could have lasted several weeks will now last just forty-five minutes by air. Such is the power of technology and the promotion of laziness.

Christians are not stopping at the laziness that society and technology offer them; they are also importing it into the body of Christ. For instance, we know of the old-time religion where people kneel to pray. I wonder how many Pentecostal Christians ever kneel to pray these days. Standing before the altar to present your tithe is no longer necessary. You can remain sitting and make your payment through an online transfer. Attending services and church programs is no longer particularly important; you can view programs on your handset while dozing away without fully concentrating on the proceedings. It is a risky line for modern-day Christianity to tread.

Worse still, the level of laziness in modern-day Christianity has eaten deeper than the considered superficial points above. Prayer meetings have become a no-no for many modern Christians. Asked to lead prayers for forty minutes, over thirty minutes will be spent singing. Singing is so much easier for them than praying.

Some Christians don't carry their Bible to church anymore; it is now too heavy; they instead read the Bible from their phone. While a tab may be better, you can take notes and mark areas of the scripture on your tab, etc.; a phone usually does not offer the same functions. The use of phones has now become the order of the day. Another interesting development is the attitude of modern-day Christians towards fasting. While fasting was a prerequisite for receiving power from on high in the past, the story is different today. Many modern-day Christians will eat all day and still expect power to come from heaven. No wonder our altars no longer carry fire.

Mark 9:25-29 (KJV): When Jesus saw that the people came running together, he rebuked the foul spirit, saying unto him,

Thou dumb and deaf spirit, I charge thee, come out of him, and enter no more into him. And the spirit cried, and rent him sore, and came out of him: and he was as one dead; insomuch that many said, He is dead. But Jesus took him by the hand, and lifted him up; and he arose. And when he was come into the house, his disciples asked him privately, Why could not we cast him out? And he said unto them, This kind can come forth by nothing, but by prayer and fasting.

In the above narration, the disciples of Jesus Christ could not cast out the demon in a possessed child. They were surprised at the ease with which Jesus cast the demon out of the child. They then approached him to know why they could not cast the demon out.

Jesus told them it is not about prayer alone, but it must go with fasting. A careful look at the two keywords could also reveal something of interest to Christians. We usually hear "Fasting and prayer" because we see it as a big deal when it comes to fasting. Many then concentrate on fasting without much thought for a prayer, which is as good as a hunger strike.

The way Jesus puts it is what I find fascinatingly different. He said, "Prayer and fasting." In other words, prayer is still the primary factor; communication with God is still the principal thing, but then adding fasting makes a difference.

Fasting becomes a necessary adjunct to prayer to receive power from on high, perform miracles and wonders, and go beyond the usual. Fasting should return to our service to God and should not be a once-in-a-year event.

As a result of the new unfortunate trend of evading anything we perceive as stressful in our society, and even in our service to God, the new generation of Christians are young, lazy Christians who want to have all things easy. They consider giving serious thought to what to wear to church as an unnecessary burden.

The result is a generation of pastors who preach what people want to hear rather than what the Spirit of God has to say. They preach the gospel of "Come as you are, it is allowed." Everything is allowed, from crazy hairstyle to dress sense rivaling that of lunatic and crazy behavior in church coupled with no regard for the place called the altar. Many 'tolerant' pastors now use the pulpit to put people in the pit rather than pull them out of the hole. They do not preach the soul's salvation or heaven and hell's existence. Since they only preach what people want to hear, they preach about blessings and victory over unseen enemies.

The unfortunate situation creates the perfect breeding ground for the present generation of false prophets who key into the laziness of the present-day, mostly young Christians. These false prophets preach that you do not have to work for God in person; all you need is to send in your money. While using your money for the work of God is good, showing up and getting involved is better.

The false prophets also prophesy about certain enemies seeking the lives of their victims and promise to pray to God on their behalf. All they must do again is send in the money. Then they go a bit further by saying certain enemies of their victims are too strong, and fasting will be required. Again, they agree to fast on one condition; send in the money. While the Bible encourages a personal relationship with God, these false men of God preach a third-party kind of relationship.

These wicked false prophets who worship their belly rather than God only capitalize on the laziness of the present generation of Christians. They see their weakness and promptly key into it, causing confusion among their congregation.

Interestingly, they claim to be fasting for the members of their fold for money but eat more than their followers and do not fast at all. They claim to fast daily but have huge pot bellies while their congregation continues to lose weight.

These lazy Christians, who are too lazy to pray, fast, or read the Bible, soon become enslaved to the false prophets. They end up being manipulated by the false prophets. Many of them have been destroyed by these horrible false prophets.

Another level of laziness in the present generation of Christians is that the time for service to God is when they have something important to do. After all, they can contract their prayer and fast to another; how about their worship too? They pay into the church account in the name of one thing or the other.

When these lazy men and women are called to join the ushering department, they say they cannot stand for long. When invited to join the evangelism group, they claim they do not want to be exposed to the elements. When asked to join the Sunday school department, they claim they do not have time to study. When asked to join the children's department, they confess they do not have tolerance for children. They are not ready to be valuable to God in any way. All they want is sweet talks from their pastor, who continue to fool them into 'sending in the money.'

John 16:33 (KJV) says These things I have spoken unto you, that in me ye might have peace. In the world ye shall have tribulation: but be of good cheer; I have overcome the world.

Tribulation comes to all. Either born again Christian or not. As expected, when trials come to these lazy Christians, they do not manage them well. Some of them question God for allowing tribulation to come their way simply because of their dull understanding of the word of God. Others leave the faith or seek alternative solutions to the challenges before them. The final result is often losing their salvation and going after other gods for help. Their laziness eventually paves a path for them to go to hell.

Study to shew thyself approved unto God, a workman that needeth not to be ashamed, rightly dividing the word of truth. 2 Timothy 2: 15 (KJV).

Poor understanding of the word of God and its relevance is a significant undoing of these lazy Christians. This generation never has a better time to turn a new leaf. The time to return to the foot of the cross is now.

2 Timothy 2:4 (KJV) says, "No man that warreth entangleth himself with the affairs of this life; that he may please him who hath chosen him to be a soldier."

Every Christian is a soldier in the body of Christ. Therefore, every soldier of God is expected to set his mind on spiritual rather than carnal things. He is expected to shun laziness and embrace service in the vineyard of God.

1 John 2:15-17 (KJV) emphasizes, *"Love not the world, neither the things that are in the world. If any man love the world, the love of the Father is not in him.*

"For all that is in the world, the lust of the flesh, and the lust of the eyes, and the pride of life, is not of the Father, but is of the world.

"And the world passeth away, and the lust thereof: but he that doeth the will of God abideth forever."

The message is to leave the world and return to God. Laziness has no place in Christ, and every child of God is expected to rise and shine through the darkness of the present world.

The last stanza of a famous hymn goes thus
Then in fellowship, sweet
We shall sit at His feet
Or we'll walk by His side in the way
What He says we will do
Where He sends, we will go
Never fear only trust and obey

As a matter of urgency, every child of God must develop a relationship with God. The walk with God is not something to delay; the time to take those first few baby steps is now. Those baby steps soon lead to bold mature steps in Christ.

Start your walk with Him now.

"This I say then, Walk in the Spirit, and ye shall not fulfill the lust of the flesh.

"For the flesh lusteth against the Spirit, and the Spirit against the flesh: and these are contrary the one to the other: so that ye cannot do the things that ye would" Galatians 5: 16 (KJV).

Walking in the Spirit is one way of eliminating fleshly lust and laziness. The better our walk with God, the smoother our stand in Him. The stronger our effort to know God, the more He draws us close to himself.

"And when Abram was ninety years old and nine, the LORD appeared to Abram, and said unto him, I am the Almighty God; walk before me, and be thou perfect" Genesis 17:1 (KJV).

Abraham was ninety years old when God called and told him to walk before Him in perfection. It is never too late to start that walk with God. Many people feel they have gone too far in the wrong direction to return, but it is never too late to start doing it right.

Many people in the church are over fifty but have never been in any department in church. They have never experienced serving God in a unit within the body of Christ. While it is ignorance for some, it is a result of laziness for others and going through a lazy spiritual system prevalent in most churches today. Even at age ninety, you can start your walk with God. It is never too late to begin your journey into eternal glory. It will be a disaster to go through life, claim to be a

Christian but fail to make heaven at the end of it all. This is the time to earn your stars and secure a place in heaven.

Another aspect of laziness is the refusal to take physical action; many people would instead pray for a job and not take the necessary step to develop themselves to qualify for the job. They would instead pray for a financial breakthrough but not try to search for creative ways to make money. The best way to generate wealth is to provide value and solve problems. Many will not challenge themselves to action; there is nothing bad with praying, but we must learn to pray hard like we never worked and work like we never prayed. Shun laziness, shun other gods, start your walk with God, and you will never regret it. God bless you as you do.

Conclusion

What saddens me most about these false Preachers' activities is how they have kept people in bondage; they rule people's lives like modern-day enslavers. The enslavers of the old days are better than them because they do not come like friendly people. Still, these false preachers appear like good people who want to help you in one way or the other, but what they do is keep their gullible followers in bondage, if possible, forever. They do not have a conscience; they have the support of their spouses and family members to perpetuate their evil deeds. They have increased the number of mental illnesses in society. As I emphasized earlier, the most important thing is for people to have a personal relationship with God. Do not look for an earthly mediator or a third party; God wants us to have direct access to Him through Jesus Christ our Lord. He has given us the privilege to connect with Him directly. We do not need go-betweens to speak to God on our behalf. Don't get me wrong; there's nothing wrong with having someone who can offer spiritual counsel. However, you must be sure you are dealing with the right person, not the one who enjoys exploiting people. Their tactic is to create fear in the lives of their members or followers; they make it look like people will not be able to function without them; they want to be part of every decision you make, and they find a way to control your thought process and dictate what you should do. They disconnect people from their loved ones just for them to take total control.

False Preachers, in most cases, do not preach salvation from their pulpits; they say many irrelevant things, convert their pulpits into a place of entertainment, and are more interested in entertaining people than saving their souls.

Just imagine the pain of trusting someone to give you solace, and they end up causing you pain by lying. They tell people what they think they want to hear; most even use magical powers to control people under them. You listen to them preaching lies such as you must sow seed to make heaven. Giving is important and is vital for the propagation of the gospel but has nothing to do with you making heaven.

In my view, if you worship under a false preacher, whatever you do there is a waste of time. Money and resources spent in such places are a waste because God is not there.

Jeremiah 29:13, James 4:8, Hebrew 13:5, and Matthew 28:20; all these Bible verses explain what the presence of God feels like, and you don't get such worshiping under a false preacher.

We need to know that we cannot hold those false preachers responsible for any misfortune because the Bible tells us how to identify them and even advises us to stay away from them. Still, when you are not sensitive enough to identify them and then move away from them, you are responsible for yourself individually for failing to have a personal relationship with your God and not keeping to his instruction.

If, as a person, you aid and abet their deceptive activities, you are liable to partake in the punishment of destruction that awaits them unless you confess your sins and reconcile with your God.

False Preachers usually emphasize donations more than they would salvation; they will tell people to donate money to open doors for their blessings. Some say people should donate money to create access or open doors to heaven. A donation, or giving, has nothing to do with making heaven; asking people to donate to make heaven is like asking them to buy their way to heaven. It is imperative to know that God does not care about what you give as a requirement to make heaven; if you give all your income and do not worship God correctly, such given is not acceptable; it is more like a waste. God only cares about your heart and your walk with Him.

It is not about the giving as such but the motive; the donation should be done with good intentions and given to ministries presided over by genuine clergymen; otherwise, it would be a waste of resources.

I appeal to you, brothers, to watch out for those who can cause divisions and create obstacles contrary to the doctrine that you have been taught, avoid them. Romans 16:17

Apostle Paul advised us to avoid them because fellowshipping under false preachers can destroy lives; it is best to stay away from them.

I appeal to you, brothers and sisters, to watch out for those who cause divisions and create obstacles contrary to the doctrine you learned; avoid them. For such persons do not serve our Lord Jesus Christ but their appetites, and by smooth talk and flattery, they deceive the hearts of the naive. People need to know that they are responsible for their ignorance;

we are all expected to listen and live by the word of God.

The government measures must be proactive and take legislative actions against these charlatans. They need to be stopped as their actions continue to destroy souls. They must be held accountable and made to pay for every wrong deed, including sexual harassment and financial exploitation. People should know that the anointing of God is not on such people and hence does not deserve respect and commitment. RUN AWAY FROM THEM.

We need to ensure that we do not have quack pastors anymore; there are no quack chaplains. Therefore, Pastors who want to manage the souls and emotions of people should be well-trained before starting a ministry.

Pastoral services need some regulation; it is not enough to just come out and "say God told me" Countries like Rwanda do not allow someone without Theological training to establish a church.

Is it appropriate to expose them? Yes, it is a sin to aid their activities; they should be exposed, as stated in Ephesians 5:11.

My primary interest is the liberation of souls under them; I sincerely hope people have the courage to detach themselves from such preachers.

When your Church becomes a burden, you are not in the right place; you are responsible for your actions. Such as failure to identify and expose them even while knowing all the evil they commit.

The false preachers, if their activities are not brought under control, there will be a revolution against even the genuine ones; I propose that the government do something before it's too late.

You must identify them by their fruits, expose their deeds and flee from them; no one will do that for you.

Identify them, expose them, and run. Not to run in fear but to separate yourself. I know that people can build close relationships with God like their earthly father and still enjoy all the good benefits of being with God.

Let me make myself an example; what led me to Christ was when I was extremely sick with Chronic Pneumonia, my medications were not working, and it felt like I was going to die. I could not sleep at night because I was in pain, the chest ache so bad, I could not breathe normally, I would open my mouth to catch my breath, and when I coughed, the room would stink. One afternoon my mum was crying and asking God to spare my life, that she couldn't afford to lose two children in her lifetime; she never knew I was hearing her; she thought I was sleeping. After she left, I pleaded with God to spare my life and promised to serve him if he gave me another chance to live.

After that, I noticed improvements, and in a few days, I got better; it took me weeks to fully recover, and I did recover and forgot my commitment, so I went back to my everyday life.

About 25 years ago, while watching 700 Club, a TV show on Christian Network, I listened to some true-life stories; in the process, I remembered that I had not kept my promise to God even though he saved my life. So, I decided to keep my promise, instantly confessed my sins, and accepted Christ in my life on December 4th, 1997; that was how the journey began.

My main message here is that I was not led to Christ in the presence of any preacher as it is usually done; not long after that, I received instructions from the Holy Spirit. Everyone can know God, serve Him, and build a strong relationship with Him without a third party.

About the Author

Oladipupo Jude Mesole is from Ponyan, Yagba East Local area of Kogi State, North Central region of the Federal Republic of Nigeria, West Africa, and a Yoruba by ethnicity.

He is a Software Engineer with vast experience in Information Technology across Banking, communications, transportation, and oil and gas.

He is a certified Christian Chaplain of Christ Life Chaplaincy Institute in Brooklyn, New York. He is involved in encouraging people and counseling them on dealing with life issues through Christian doctrines.

Mesole graduated from the Federal University of Technology, Minna, with B. Tech in Physics/Telecommunications Technology in 2006 (Nigeria). He attended the University of East London and obtained an MSc in Computer Systems Engineering (Software Systems) in 2013 (UK).

He attended Christ-life Bible Institute & Seminary Brooklyn, New York (USA) and graduated in 2020 with a Doctor of Theology (Th.D.)

Mesole obtained a PGP in Data analytics from Purdue University Indiana in 2022 (USA) and is currently undertaking a Ph.D. in Communications at Liberty University, Virginia, USA.

Mesole is a Certified SAP SD Business process Consultant (Waldorf Germany) 2014, Certified Data analyst in Analytics

Foundation, Python Programming, R Language for Data Science, Tableau for Data Visualization. (2021-2022)

He is married to Oluyemisi Mesole and blessed with two children, Joel Oluwashina Mesole and Oladipupo Joshua Mesole.

www.ingramcontent.com/pod-product-compliance
Lightning Source LLC
Chambersburg PA
CBHW062038120526
44592CB00035B/1243